Love in the Time of Plague

THE WILD LILY INSTITUTE

IBSN *978-1-387-70021-9*

First Edition: First Printing 2022

Cover design and interior layout: Voetelle Art & Design
Cover Image: Canva premium License. Used by Permission.

Published by:

 Potter's Press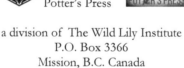

a division of The Wild Lily Institute
P.O. Box 3366
Mission, B.C. Canada
V2V 4J5
www.wildlilyinstitute.com

Love in the Time of Plague

Emily Isaacson

Potter's Press
Vancouver

Dedicated to

Edward

Let me know when you begin the new tea,
and the new white wine.
My present elegances have not yet made me
indifferent to such matters.
I am still a cat if I see a mouse.

—*Jane Austen*, Letter to Cassandra

The spiritual way ruins the body and, having ruined it,
restores it to prosperity:
Ruined the house for the sake of the golden treasure, and
with that same treasure builds it better than before;
Cut off the water and cleansed the river-bed, then
caused the drinking water to flow in it;
Cleft the skin and drew out the barb, then made fresh
skin grow over the wound;
Razed the fortress and took from it the infidel, then
reared thereon a hundred towers and ramparts.

—*Rumi*

Contents

Medieval Apothecary

The Apothecary's Daughter

At the apothecary shop
is the crossroads of medieval medicine,
where change is of the essence,
and time stands alone.

She is young, she is strong with laughter,
and her will is steady;
her hazel eyes speak of healing
her lips are a rose, speaking in the wind,
her hands are as skillful as the land,
the tonic bends beneath her hands,
vials and ointments
are scepters extended to the poor and ill:
she is the apothecary's daughter.

Carnelian—
her face is flax damask,
as she travels with a cowl over her head
through the cloister's silence dead,
she carries the crude anthracite
to her father's benefactor's rite.

The children play in burgundy knickers
around the fountain,
but she is as silent as dawn
and threading doves,
as the far-away gallop of hooves
on a crusade.

"I can turn a thistle to a daffodil in a day,"
said the passing alchemist
with a wry smile,
"and the rain becomes
crystals beneath my hand.
My skull is made of wood, not clay."

"What creates the connection
between the roses
are the thorns,"
said the apothecary's daughter.
"For you are an illusionist,
and I am Carnelian,
the thorn of perdition."

"Hold it to your lantern glass,
for you are a rose—
(I do not want the roses to be without
stems or leaves or thorns…)"
said the alchemist.
"Through the glass is a light,
and beneath my heart
there is a country—
you have found the Door!"

"Alas," she paused,
"if there is a country within you,
there is an empire
within me—"

"What empire? Apothecary's daughter,"
he asked with a jeer,
"What empire protects you?"

"Why it is the empire of the royal rose,"
she stood her ground.
He looked through his spectacle at her closely:
"The royal rose that entwines the golden arbour—
is that the empire of which you speak?"

"It is an aged rose
from which steeps
the sweet perfume of roses' oil,
as I would know,"
she answered.
"Then be assured
that I not only
know the secret of the rose,
but the place from which it sprang—
that would make a maiden weep."

"I weep as surely
as I live, if I do not know
the medicine of the gorse, the heather,
and of the rose:
it springs from
the rose hip,
and is a woman's remedy.
Now, I must be off,
for my smokeless coal
is growing dim
before my eyes—" she said.

Aha! thought the alchemist—
the lady did not know that
we would meet,
for until now I could only dream
of her medicine
to make a woman sweet.

The arched passage rang
with his voice,
for he scarce cared to lower it.
"Your father knows both
his friends and benefactors,"
he said, "but does he know his enemies?"

"Pray tell, who is his enemy?"
she asked. "There is a robin perched
on his chestnut bud."
"Why his enemy is anyone who,
with skill, is cunning
and works to undermine him," he said.
"What is within the human heart, will
eventually flower after its own kind,
for it cannot stay hidden very long.

"If, a dance," he said, taking her hand,
"it must be worked out
as a sequence of steps,
while dripping with sweat."

"The life without it, though,
is passionless," she said.

"Toil in the valleys
of the human heart
for happiness is hard to find,
and when we find it
we let go all too soon.

"We breathe and spin
and leap—our faith in our mouths,
our life lived with one last
mournful cry," he said.

They had met at last—
a chance meeting:
"And what is your name?" she asked.
"Waterford," he answered.

"Waterford, the son of crusaders?" she asked.
"Yes, and keeper of the Waterford Journal—
for I can write," he said.
"You may not remember me,
but I was in your benefactor's school
as a child. Do you remember I sent you a note?"

"Aye," said Carnelian, "but I could not read it."

"I will tell you what it said," he answered.

"Do not despise thou love, nor rue its share,
the shelter it provides is providence,
the elegance of home is free from cares,
and thine bent head in prayer is evidence.
I have many flowers in my garden,
each smells so sweetly of the summer's air,
envelopes of colour, secret wardens,
for all the trust that heav'n keeps guarded there.
If ever I should give my heart to one,
I would find her 'neath an arbour waiting;
my intimations second to her none,
there'd be one song in my mouth abating:
I would give thee my youth's flattery now
that I may not prove false upon thy vow."

"I remember now," said Carnelian.
"Then you were last to read it," he said.

"Last was I to read your cream folded note,
when I was still quite young, I would not laugh
at your sincerity, and my wood staff.
My reputation was my ivory throat.
I would take you at your word, upon sea
I float: saline is my buffer, salt pure
that reaches deep into my wounds, censured
as crystalline mine salt, deep in the green,
we move, we float, licensed liquidity.
And now the years have almost passed me by,
I remember you, the boy that once kythed
in books and music, gardens' flow'r to me.
Do not let me forget the passing age,
that once held me, a player, on the stage."

Old Poets

Battersea Bridge

In the middle,
cold and the wind,
howling
over the
parapet,
dark and
lifeless,
broken into
a crumpling
of dreams,
about to
consume despair
or gratitude.

Laughter at Oxford

One late
afternoon, poet
sanding away
at a nobler journey,
leaves drifting
into later pools
that drip
with years,
of bare wood
floors, mute…

One bench sings
with stolen youth:
romance, hushed,
staring out
under the cascade
of gentleness.

To An Aged Don

Dear sir,
from "The Taste of
Pineapple: A Basis for Literary
Criticism,"
your "emphasis
on the quiddity
of things"
sustains your star-darts
in the heavens
as we wait for
the Most Holy
Sacrament,
buoyant
upon the flames
of civilization.

Of a War

Staring down the
gallows,
barrels of clouds,
rifling on the
horizon
into the next
lesson of mankind's
brutal frame:
the floating of
conception
(steeped in glory):
a charge and banner.

Crown of Thorns

You who consumed
all humanity's
brokenness
in one crushed
cross—
a crown of thorns
yet perched
on the brow
of a Jewish carpenter;
simple are your
currents, blowing
against the night,
against the star-splattered
sky.

Meditations in a Flame

Captive to my
merchants
in the eye of the
aurora,
eclipsed into eternity—
warers and vendors,
stumbling over
the dogs,
skewed among the flames;
each fruit, from a blossom,
each having torn a leaf.

O cross of thorns:
how desperate is your
eye, unseen,
in the voice of his dying.

Eye of the Storm

Crucified
in deep suspicion,
the wreck
harboured deep
beneath the gold.
In squalid liberty,
we candidly
renounce
(beneath the rancour),
your deep black and
white
criticism.

Quill and Ink

Under witticism,
rifling through
old
pages,
charitable with poetic
intent,
the flower garden watered
and green
with honour, incense,
insight, wonders, terrors
of a poet's soul...

Overhead,
the roses,
translucent-white
to crown you—
the verse so sweet
with summer, rung
over the hills
of down.

In Prison

The magical impulse,
architectured
in latent
realms,
solaced by
cement—
we dance,
inebriated at the
bare bars of
hell's gate—
aching for nothing,
walking the floors
white as lead,
like tulips buried
beneath the snow:
the moon,
a madonna.

Emeritus

On a platform,
smocked,
daintily sketching
your wildflower
haloes and prism
eyes—
cornflower blue,
ceramic sky
falling out of
heaven and Atlantis.

Shepherds,
we encircle
our flock,
devoid of the
six eyes
of a cherubim's wing:
flattered and frail.

Walk Amongst the Shrines

Gravestones,
heaped with rubble—
all our transcendent
incantations
steeped
over the fires,
mourning the
ethereal night-green
boy
burning
charcoal against the
fragile, lost.

The River

Westward
on the floats,
winding downriver
transpired
under the nets
of dark-haired women.

The train floats by,
its trestle rain-shook
and wintery;
the mosaic of
water-bright
fish eyes,
giddy
among the wild grass.

Where the moon
is harnessed under
the sky,
over the white
slat-board church,
a eunuch
carries his mother,
still bright,
like a lotus
blooming
under the bile sun.

Farm Boy

Taking the pickaxe
to a pile of wood
for one day of
November, the cold
and frost
icing the tree limbs,
firewood piled in the
foyer.

Swinging the
bucket,
lashing from the pump
one morning's worth
of tea:
our herbs
in all flavours,
we fall into the pansies,
too simple for a bath.

Chronicle

Under
the shadows
of old bookstore dust,
shaded and bleary-eyed,
having drunk
an ounce of ruby tea
in an old stone cup;
your velvet cape,
an eloquent verse,
the gallows,
stacks reaching into
thin air—
their ebullient glory,
a page leaf.

Folds of a flapper's
dress, still
sequined, between
the tissue
in an
olive wood chest.

Caravan

One thatched roof,
a sprinkling of
firs into the forest,
gypsies
light their terra-cotta
lanterns
in vibrant hue,
gold glittering in the
salty dust,
among the peasant feet,
worn,
washed in the basins
of the world.

Bombs and Gallows

In the mountains of the sun,
camped in the open field,
the moon was fiery red…

Looking up in the night,
at a million eyes
whistling in the darkness,
cows braying at the smoke,
the river's song in pewter,
the grass, like garlands;
still, in the dampened reeds
of Gabriel's grace.

The shattering of
black hail,
into the nestling of
wild roses,
oboes screeching
in the decks, your lacy
fingers at our throats—
we laid the cards,
black queen, black heart,
one club, one spade,
for a game of parlour.

Draped in wine,
we cross the sky,
flourish through the night,
and mark our
marble epitaphs.

Shetland Pony

The country:
blueberry wine,
white and blue
china on the
vine-encroached table,
hyacinths streaked
with water,
cream-coloured
cloths layered
under the peasant feast;
wood-lacquered baskets
blooming,
in navy and
petal-white.

Winding
out beneath us,
the roads that
disappear...
we go on,
the horses trotting,
on and on;
the lights
in the distance,
soft noses, in velvet,
on and on.

Gold Vermilion

Ethan,
ever after referred
to as an open-ended
conversationalist,
heavy-witted,
sold on a prospect,
like a fine gladiator
swinging a heavy sword,
amid the nursery-tale
treasury in Flan.
Straight-edged silver
with long curls
reaching to his
sword-hilt,
swung for battle;
horses
in the Parthenon,
striped,
blue and gold,
and liqueur,
like chocolate
brandy.

Dante

In the still
mist world,
the inner chambers
of the
moon unworn,
inlaid with
clarity, smoked—
ringless
in your stormy eyes,
one unicorn
leaps from
the falls…

Nuns chanting,
haunting
the fall,
the early autumn,
paisley:
one olive tree
in plain song,
plaited hair
bound
with ribbons.

Motet

Dryads melting into
infernos, deaf
with self-pity, caked in
pig's manure,
vile with rage;
streaming with blood,
the sylphs, a silent
movement, white and black
ravens and pawns
draped in flour sacks,
the silver cuff links
in the library.

Clutching a wire
harem, veering
to the left, esteemed
delphinium,
like pumpernickel
in a cool,
dark closet
with the dead-of-night
rats.

Valentine Raptures

The red door
swung open,
unsuspecting
of the left-handed
visitor,
crocheted squares like
the breezes…

In hearts and roses,
willowing
our tresses
into love-knots.

Ballet

The night drew a silent line
in the theatre against
the thunderous audience,
the orchestra paused in the pit,
the violin's resonant soprano
an elite comprehension,
and the conductor metered
the seconds.

The dance hung on
the verge
of worlds;
each adagio, the measure
of a moment
with or without beauty's resin
and the demarcation
of mystique.

The crinoline swished
with toe shoes en pointe,
en pirouette
across the floor rubbed
a solemn pattern—
arabesque, the nightingale
of soft-spoken moments,
and a choreographed
future to mimic poise.

The Poet

In panes,
under the candles of the sky,
ladled like soup to the common
and poor, who
adrift—
rage their dreams
and sonnets
crease the night.

Back from the death,
all story spiwery,
hangs
its cloak,
wick in its covering
by the fire,
the beautiful,
cradled
in her peace.

The Bread

Leavened,
the oven parches
and prepares
the sacred loaf to
dry perfection.

Piece by piece, torn
into white segments,
to participate with
wine
in sorrow and suffering,
in forgiveness and repentance—

And rebirth,
knowing our hostile hearts
he came,
and the direction of his love
is an endless
source, repeating the grace
of a moment in time,
forever.

Acacia

One pearl
among the blackberry
leaves, amid
pine and field—
African lace
blowing in the whitened
breeze,
over the clank
of steel.

Three children play
under the
tangle-wood bed
and the yellow
halls
resound
with whales and
cabbages
underfoot.

The garden of arugula,
downwind;
laughter
and I
part shaded,
amongst the
mornings.

Pale Lights

One moon,
reflected in
a shallow pool,
like a seashell
in a foreign sky,
azure,
her skirts swirled,
garnet
under the night—
her silk like
corn, burnished
over coals,
and water,
too pure
to drink.

Old Worlds

Crocus under
the magnolia,
spotted white and gold,
gentle lions
cross my path,
pawing and roaring,
the sun falling out
of heaven
into the sepulchral orbit
of gentle kings
and strong queens,
reminiscent
of the river's mouth,
and an orchard
by the ruins
of an old castle.

Other Suns

In the seventh
constellation
of the milky way,
Neptune,
through a sword,
brandished in jest,
Jupiter,
jumping in
and out of well pools,
Saturn,
spell-deep:
Earth,
resilient and verdant,
Venus,
resplendent
as wildflowers
over Olympia,
Mars,
salient as
breaking oceans' roar,
Uranus's eagles
swift
in eventide,
Pluto,
a simple salutation,
and Mercury-white coals,
a thousand years
into the dawn.

Other Galaxies

On the garden
bench,
the auburn head
bent over the violin,
sun-glazed
skirts, fading
navy and lilac
in the shadows;
the melon balls on plates,
the shawls of lace,
memories like tulle
around the
miniature horses.

Crushed ice
and a maraschino cherry—
you had one good hat,
and wore it
with a jaunt;
your coat,
combed black wool,
your dark hair
hidden under
a lacquer of fortes.

Peacocks
strutting
over the lawn:
little cherubs
in the terraced gardens,
running down to
the stream's pale
violet haunt.

Chrysanthemum

Glowing hot coffee,
your eyes,
walking on coals,
drinking
your
cream, crushed
from vine-ripened
destiny.

From the white sea,
sand-dollars deep
on the deep bottom
of clarity,
where my feet
touch
you gently,
gently touch you,
our seahorses,
dried and brittle.

Stone Fortress

One summer's night,
the old library,
mahogany,
emerald light
at dusk
mapping the long tables
of silent students—

Studying
the water carrier,
the ram, the eagle,
the unicorn, the serpent,
the dove, the wolf,
the centaur, the whale
under a handful
of stars, sacred and
rock-silent in a cradle—

Each constellation's lullaby
re-seeding the fields
of night, with fixity
a counterpoint
to variable destiny.

The moon, a wide mouth,
swallowing
the seas of darkness.

Hearth Fire

In the cold, smooth North,
under the sharp ring of
winter solstice,
knee-deep in novels,
four children deep
in dreams,
like monks in books,
we pull them from the world's
seashells, unbroken—

Willow tree ornaments
shored like driftwood
on the mantle, each
one an elusive olive-skinned
vagabond.

Shining Armour

Arms crossed
on the old wooden bench;
hair, lithe
in a breeze.

Summer-browned,
with curled skins
in pools
around your ankles,
pared for pie;
the apple tree,
a hearty son at dusk,
the soft-wood
house ruffled
like eyelet
amongst the trees...
a sonatina child,
its shining
whisperer.

Elegies

From The Ashes of Notre Dame

I crossed myself and stood at the altar,
eternity wound around my finger:
the crushed moment of my solemn singer
was the moment when the burned stone faltered.
I cannot ask for more from Gibraltar,
but for one of these little ones, ringer
of the bells that call them home, rise linger
on the sweetened isle, fading light loiters
as the peals repeat and resound, silence
breaking at the notion of sound's fury.
The burnished cathedral has fallen, died;
attic to cellar smoke with violence,
the steeple tied to the dead we bury
when the beating steel heart of Paris cried.

Notre Dame's Last Singer

Our Lady, you are our noblest hero,
we swing our incense smoke for your reply
from the paradise in which you supply
our needs and our commands, how blithely so
do we insist on our own proven low
calculations, buying time on earth by
earning sterile bleak favours from God. My
home torn asunder with each gothic blow,
I was on my knees now to watch the fire
bludgeon the sky with inhuman cruelty.
We sang as city incarnadine burned,
with its altruistic Catholic spire;
we wept as Christ's face in ash was beauty,
as against us the broken stone face turned.

Song of the Volta

I was divine and now I am far gone:
burned beyond recognition and accused,
left for dead as once broken and abused,
I am left with the carcass and the stone.
The chalk of my skull likely stays beyond
the years of torment and the hours of pain,
the old earth never washed away by rain,
the ancient sin not acquiesced by blood.
My innocence never belonged to me—
so can it sin? Oh can it anguished burn?
I thought to be a lovely lamb, as snows;
spring in the dun heather and the moss peat.
My towering hulk flew toward skies and churned
that the red blood has frozen in my rose.

Proverbial Contusions

Dance, dance as though the world had played a card,
we are one body, one corps the wind moves;
we ascend when we succumb to the grooves
of higher beings, engraved oils of nard.
The precious tree became the oil and hard
as diamonds the covenant makes deep blue,
my skin has turned as cold as the dead's hue,
and still I am steaming your dark Swiss chard.
There was a moment when I doubted you:
I saw you as a distant politeness.
But now your hand has clasped my arm in life
and I die no more, I lie in ruins too:
you are my golden child of plaid kindness—
and I rush on, rising amid the strife.

Mentor's Last Rite

My long ornate arms stretched to take you in,
hands welcoming with hospitality—
into the realm of Christ's divinity.
You put your two coins in the church of tin.
I ran the race of life to gaining, win,
you ran beside on personality;
tell he who made the robin and the tree
there was one more touch of madness or sin,
you would walk no more, nor truant-wing fly;
your vestal wounds had all been scavenged, seared,
there was little left to love but a shell.
Priests would say your last rites lest you faithless die,
though the church's holy altar once was feared,
you walk into Christ's silvered arms full well.

The Lost Church

Where have you gone, my little flock of sheep;
have you dispersed over the Vosges's pass?
Have you stayed to another river's glass?
Have you fallen down a gully so steep?
Where is the sacrament that with you keeps
you from death's harm, and with your greenest grass:
a pastureland of Liseron des Champs,
the pleasant place where White Asphodel steeps.
I wish you had waited for your shepherd,
I, standing in the ruins of the lost,
did not see you go, nor will you to leave.
The procession for my missing, a dirge,
I singing, naive of the wind's frost
on the autumn backdrop of burnished leaves.

Morning in the Burned Cathedral

The light streams through, alas it is morning—
I cannot bear the truth in its meaning,
for I have lost my life's most precious thing:
and with it I am wrought 'till evening.
I bear the brunt of tragedian's telling,
I'd not want to be the soul's recounted fling
with crown jewels, and buried sages' grieving
over lost moments, proverbs still singing.
There is a moment when I contemplate—
and all meaning fades in the trenches of France,
and all I love resounds, hollow as wine
no more in a chalice, bread on a plate.
My breakfast, ashes of Petite Pervenche:
wildflowers over the fields of its kind.

Have I Loved Death?

It is true I loved my enemy death,
black to my white, the err to my person,
the assailant to humanity's son;
my grievance with death is it only perfects
those it loves—makes them pale, protects
them from the harsh rays of the yellow sun,
never shall they burn, cripples those who run,
all you held dear will then calloused defect.
There is a burnished French Horn at the end
when you reach the Hallmark mansion, the lake,
and the Canada geese's wild call to you.
Here you tidy rest, hands folded, you bend
to the one faded cloth copy of Blake
on the table, the piano is tuned.

Wild Grass of France

I collected the wildflowers and sent
them in letters to my love long lost,
I was a soldier in France, grass in frost
froze in all withered directions, bent,
there was a wind that with it, fragranced, lent
its luminous hue, its sharp brittle cost,
and to its tune a piper's Pentecost—
its denial of any resistance.
It bent the winter trees, they greenly sang,
it bent the nectar spring in maritime,
it bent the gardens of Primrose-blue fleurs—
wind, the sea roared, the salt, the sanguine rang;
it braved the Charente coast of ocean's thyme.
I guarded your heart like an art oeuvre.

Millefleurs

The alpine meadows are spun with millefleurs
and forests of pine, beech, and poplar rend
all of France fragrant, now nuanced, and send
my poems like tiny birds heavenwards.
Wrought iron slants in afternoon and mars
the manicured green's magic haunt, lend
me the whisper for a moment of a thousand
prayers 'round the property's pristine scars,
the battle wounds have gored the trench:
there are cold gashes in the weathered wood.
Light through old lace at the windows' black frame,
the thunderous sky's tenuous grey drench
down clouds scuttling past—broom-coloured oak stood
on hillsides, a missive of gated fame.

Have I Loved Life?

I was a Blue Rock Thrush that sang outside
the Louvre, for the art made my throat swell
and the Boreal Owl descended well
into night. Bohemian Waxwing bride
flew a trousseau the size of lengthy wide
medieval tapestries. Dotted with miel
were croissants at the long table; the belle
danced under the long windows of Versailles.
We sang a tune, a lyric of her best
versified Monday morning room lightened
by the sun through the olive velvet drapes.
The library met her moments in rest
with long-dead poets and dames to brighten
the dark—lit wax candles, 'neath my landscapes.

Petrarchan Hymn

The last light fades, for it is winter now;
there is a thorn-pierced shore, within the cove
with waves that overlap the tides that rove
ragged with driftwood, on a distal bronze brow.
The ocean held the saline ship's bow;
beneath the salty waves the orcas dove
to sandy darkened depths of blue and mauve,
that rose to Magnificat's undertow.
And the floor threw shells of alabaster
with frequent storm and violent drenches,
the greenest land was littered now with stone.
The innocent hands of trees were master,
constant arms outstretched between two branches
made of the Virgin Mother's bluest bone.

Our Lady of the Night

She was stone and clear water flowed in shoots,
fountains of joy came from beneath her hands:
her figure, the sacred image of lands
where the Catholic tree spread its deep roots.
A vision: Fatima appeared in woods;
walkers visited almond marble bands,
the gown that was as mystical as sands
shifting in the desert. The light that should
disperse over her form and the 'spiring pines,
would glimmer in her unseeing white eyes,
and her earthly blindness unveiled the sight
of a thousand angels, ready at signs
of her distress. To her side and her sighs
of pity—the revealing of the light.

The Crucified One: Magnificat

The Renaissance would sing of you in blue
and white stained glass, with ruby crown,
the red blood of your body next ran down
to the torment of your outer flesh; you
were determined to die in every room
of the three levels of humankind: sound
doctrine made us build stone mansions, to found
hell, and earth, and heaven. Before monsoons
of spirits conjured up ideals—hours
swept away like old houses and picket
fences, marigolds flying in maize.
Rose-red smile, the dark hair, and pale-powdered
face of evening, Lilith's flow'r, Lilibet's
cry from all lands sounds, pure oil in a haze.

Isaacson's Last Hour

Hourglass

The minute grain of sand
through the hourglass, counts
each moment of me,
each person I become,
with airs or plain common sense—
You dressed me in linen,
as the wild grass burrs,
and anointed me with fine perfume
from the paisley flowers of the field;
streaming down my forehead
was your oil.

So I was cleansed from within,
so I walked free like a man
released from a prison.
The temple's gate welcomed me,
the church house sang my arias,
they trellised the treble
and reverberated the bass,
note by note.

The hourglass sand is
whiter than snow,
never runs sour,
is as multicoloured as fire,
and salty as the sea,
pouring and pouring
until it turns again.

Love Poem of the Lily

The difficulties of life cannot overcome thee,
for thou art my constant and divine.
The gilded lily speaks from a royal age,
apportioning regal kindness
as a pillar of society, while youth rage.
Here you stood on a cliff with
the wind in your hair,
you were more savage than mild,
more gilded than wild—
the wind howled,
and there was a long space.

The empire of kindness grew.
Black note. Entwined.
Grace note. Elegy. Rest.
Then everyone looked at you
and saw you were unequally yoked.
The planets and moons began to fall out of space,
and you were out of sorts,
bought a glitzy ball gown, curled your hair, twirled
as a Dowager before the waltz.

Butterfly Tears

I once said I love you
and that love remains;
constant through years,
the blood in my veins.

I never will leave you,
be I poor or of wealth,
as the sun crosses the sky,
without guile, without stealth.

And though the ashes remain of our years,
they are sacred because of our butterfly tears.

Threnody of the Thistle

(Ode to the national flower of Scotland)

Thistle manor, away off the moor,
here the thistle down blows…
and away lullaby, mother sing,
lullaby to a prince and a king.
Here there is no sense of repeat,
just a mild prickly pod bed,
enumerating the signs
of harvest to summer's end.
The trees and the heather
all lean like the wind.

Eventually the thistle down speaks—
down, down, thistle moor,
dusting o'er the creaking floor
to the stone gorse garden door:
resurgence from poverty to kin,
from ignorance to education,
forgiving liniment
from within, cold without
from the imminent
moor fog, hazing our sight.
From cradle to Yule log,
burn foolish, burn bright!

Canon of Bloom

Find a door to the garden
repository of bushels of peonies
in fiery purple as pardon,
effulgent contrast to the spicy chives,
juicy tomatoes, and spindly green beans,
continuance after the planting of seeds.
Armfuls of yellow daffodils
are a brilliant surprise at Easter.
Tulips riotous red—
each plant's colour diffuses
with the morning
and rises with the heat of afternoon.

The poplar down blew
over the back fence of
the schoolyard;
I reached for the knobby trees
as I scratched in my notebook.
Herbs, fruits, and flowers
my mother carefully planted, weeded, and pruned,
with an eye for their immortal powers.
A city could flourish beneath this hand,
with prudence. But cities would be tombs.
All for the petals of a brightened land,
canon of faithful bloom.

Burning Cinders

I listened from out the little window
to see if I could hear your song
in the lane,
and when the familiar whistle sounded,
even my dulcet heart gave way.

There was the song of us
that whistled on the moor
before the seasons began,
when we knew we'd be together
even in a foreign land.

There was the wood
that burned dry in the hearth;
I took a coin from my purse,
and counted the face on it
memorizing the moments your touch
reached out in healing.

There was the building of
something new amid the old,
a search for independence,
a need to voice a referendum.

The old country calls me home.
Its architecture has not yet crumbled.
I wave from my window
and write Scottish poems
to the sonorous bagpipe,
the fire, burning, burning cinders.

Dirge of the Daffodil

Rightly in my grief, I remain, clutching daffodils;
   fondly yours, and the author of this dirge.

Whether I roll like the sea,
or drift as the clouds,
I always know you'll come back to me.
Though the earth turn swift,
or my life decay,
I always know you'll
come home some day.

When I stood at the church,
and said my goodbye,
I knew it would not be forever,
there's a place in the sky.

Idyll of the Iris

The nacreous, mother-of-pearl cloud
between sunset and sunrise bid
the clay lie beneath the earth,
not yet formed on a potter's wheel,
illusive, waiting for a cup, a bowl, a vase,
to procure out of its shapeless form.
Yet healing emanates
where lack of dying dwells.

The bonny swan rise o'er the calm
pond swells, and iris stands straight—
a less than mediocre gate—its tear
shaped bud, from heaven descended.
Its brilliant hue, a door by which
we entered.
A woman in her fragile form
became purple iris of the morn.

True Lace of Ireland (found poem)

Kenmare lace, abloom floral, austere,
delicate, and ethereal,
altruistically made from the convent
in the tradition of the Poor Clare's.

Taken in by ardent admirers
of the antique art to preserve bright
legacy of lace by prime pupils
for posterity, using the nuns'

Original nineteenth century
pattern books, handwork and design that
flow, beautiful, each one, framed like art,
commemorative lace in a token.

The lace celebratory circle,
this year, in honour of the 150th
anniversary of Kenmare-fine
stitching, bright-bent, full-circle in time.

A Daffodil In Wales

I gave a daffodil to a homeless person once,
measuring the moment's verse into a laugh—
but he sauntered away, crushing its head
into the cool earth until its yellow disappeared.

I took a photo of the sky, watching its clouds
billow and roll, passing into eternity,
and the great wave of anguish beyond the blue
sculpted my very form into measureless light.

My skirts were the garden flowers,
my hair, the willows over the pond,
my lips were the red roses, climbing,
my neck, the white swans swimming.

I gave a daffodil to the Prince,
that he might rule Wales with a rod of iron,
and he read the verse of its heart,
and promised to love only one.

Elegy of the Royal Rose

There was always a royal rose,
in deep red hue, loyal
to a nation: entwining
as I looked deep into time.
The empire that bore
your name wore
the breastplate
with the coat of arms,
and sacred incense.

I was first to hold you,
in the lighted hour of truth,
and last to see you go,
the glisten of lush red,
the blush of pink,
a momentary trace of snow,
birth pang of departed lands—
life nestled in my open hands,
unrepentant starts,
O Commonwealth of hearts.

Letters From the Peace Tower

The Forest's Weave

At the forest's weave, the highlights flow
through wafted leaf and glistening bough,
the nectar of the flow'r, seeping breach,
it brings the tide of summer to each
sparrow, robin, blue jay, flitting bright
serious beats, rise and disappear:
unto moment shadows of the night.

I am reaching to each branch-barred heart,
starting at the absolute of ground,
now stony gowned and lush with fern, part
with the meadow in its finest hour.
The sigh of light will decorate and
stream to touch each consecrated vial:
the naturalist of rum-tainted man.

The playing tribute of another power,
willing to now rest its fated lute,
the whispering of our nature's lower
threshold, keeping time with earth's still flute.
In bold didactic strokes, and bearing
chains of poverty, without this colour:
the dawn, its early morning sterling.

Pedigree

The bright morning held its pedigree,
racing like a cool frost o'er the grass,
learning each bluebell, a memory,
leaning at the doorway of each mass,
making truth, of our hearts, the staple:
each choice the river running ragged
to silver pond with dark red maple.

Ladybug, dragonfly, hummingbird,
on minute translucent wing will fly
hovering o'er the garden of the wild;
at late noon, resounding o'er the cry
of nature, wrapped, a child at the breast:
in tattered colours of patchwork quilt,
degrading too towards the earthly rest.

The dimming light and last poignant hour
now has almost waved and said goodbye,
what sun illumined and held for power—
sweep of olden gold on fields of rye,
carving as in oak the darkening path:
we would once more raise our chant to heaven,
chasing down the solemn aftermath.

Last Light

Last light has drawn its burgundy breath
speaking through that shadowed copper tree,
gathered toward the olden curse of death—
sharp sword of fate could not now slay me.
I am host: both beauty and divine;
all who rest beneath my sojourned eaves,
travel on, akin to what is mine.

With a walking stick, and compass bared,
prayers for direction rift the heaven,
staggered under the burden of care,
took his black bread with meagre leaven,
almost fell beside the rim of road,
begotten of the music's power
yet he will stand beneath his old load.

Drawn in life to whatever you yield,
I am the fire and you are the flame;
when winging low over the red fields,
a flock of dark midnight starlings came,
flitting sparks of flight in hour of eve,
spinning their minute patterns like flax
fragile quilting of the falling leaves.

The Horizon's Muse

The larder, brimming with food and wine,
and fresh bread rising to sweet butter;
garlic tear, now minced with garden thyme,
deep marinade—to each another.
The green bean and the carrot simmer,
the venison rests immersed, scarlet,
the olive oil in the soup, a glimmer.

An apple a day glints in the sun,
the hanging branch bequeaths its quiver,
now the autumn's harvest runs
from furrow to the raging river.
Carefully plucked beneath the thorn,
blackberries stain the Devonshire cream,
eaten with a new-baked scone this morn.

The table, set with wreath of grace
spills wax from the candle in its middle,
telling the lines of your noble face,
lighting the music of your fiddle.
Our fields of corn, grow cream, row by row
into the distant horizon's muse
breaking at the ocean's foamy bow.

The Replanting

Repository, bent to worship
all the immaculate and divine
of nature, bright, bold and ladyship—
untold mountain air where all is mine,
castaway bright fields of bloom sublime,
mining in the ore of earth's last years:
my unspoken desires now define.

Heaven reaches down with painted skies,
reigning in the world and its notions—
humility flows from stormy eyes,
the presence of its highest motions.
Evil could not wield a staple sword,
nor restore destruction of our kind,
all cultivation reaching forward.

Toward the replanting of a land—
once deserted, cold, and barren, still;
now citrus, and the olive, myrtle stand,
our pride in the distance, through the hills
spilling fine perfume and virgin oil.
Early songs still rise from temple mount
amid the prayers, centuries old toil.

I Held A Lantern By The Sea

I held a lantern by the sea:
the waves crashed and roared in tempo,
the cream moon shed its light to me,
the ships, until they saw, all passed
in black darkness, the rocks amassed—
a perilous low larghetto;
the clear ocean, adagio.

I plucked a rose from fall's garden,
its sharp thorn pieced me and I wept—
on my white hand was now a scar—
if only to stay neatly kept.
Twenty roses I have gathered,
seeing not the wound of love marred,
blood-red bouquet I have tethered.

I said a prayer beside the bed,
that, in the weeping hour of lead
my spirit would rise, eternal—
pondering the moments fallow,
lessons learned upon the 'morrow,
and every spoken word transcend
while silence of the dead descend.

The Metropolitan Sun

An ingenuous clock strikes the time,
innocent lamp, on ruddy heads, shine;
naïve, wandering through books, they climb
on my knee—unworldly, pale-bright kind—
wide-eyed, turn the lucid picture page
in rustic cabin, flames of wood stove
resonate as a provincial stage.

Smart as a rainy day in left field—
high heels, lipstick, cosmopolitan
with sophisticated airs, cool meals;
won beneath the metropolitan
sun, worldly and orange in flawless bow,
the white urbanite suffrage suffice,
their collection of cars follow cows.

The gentry try their purple tailcoat,
mentoring society in wine
and charity, white as a sailboat
for nobility with a gold mine;
from aristocracy, a moment
cordiality wound itself, rose
on a lattice of elite comment.

Enclosure

The silence was my enemy;
it bound me in a prison, gray
as blocks of stone, the careful day
turned from bright to claps of thunder,
fears of silver treasure, plundered,
all of my heart laid waste in caste:
the ship with woman in its mast.

Prayer was my absolution,
a reason to leave my old home,
my journey of consolation,
the purity pearl, now to roam;
ne'er in the mirror, tarnishing,
will I see my dark enemy—
all is well, fine in polishing.

Stillness was my contemplation,
starlings pealed their veneration,
the song of night, the nightingale
sang with morose fervour, the nail
speaking of my wound forever,
telling of the writing paper
behind locked doors, in enclosure.

Cultivation Of The Olive Tree

The shoots of wild olive are grafted, born
to the cultivated tree, in the grove
where his song lingers, the breath of new morn
where the gardener walked, his mind a trove
of horticultural secrets and fruit
gifts. Who will be the chosen shoot, new green:
alabaster brow, pale, one beauty's dream.

I grew, a fruitful tree beneath his care,
his eyes watched over me in the garden,
the sorrow was not more than one can bear,
the joy of life was always in its pardon;
I was dressed in fine raiment of the white mist,
my head bore a jewelled crown of olive,
for all my days, that evil must desist.

His call echoes in the branch, innocent,
which was then taken from my garden tree
and made into a cross, the instrument
would bear a carpenter on Calvary,
beneath the darkened sun, his final vow:
forgiving all his enemies for sin,
let those the gardener grafted be brought in.

The Pigeons

The Pigeon Boxes

Pigeons flew
in grey and blue,
they rose in fluttering wing,
they clucked and wept,
they cooed and in a precise
and orderly way
the wind swept
them into the square.

There was a set of wooden boxes
on the roof—
of an oversized apartment building
that was the white colour
of a spaceship from Star Wars.
Every day the birds landed
and nestled in their boxes,
covertly denying the
measure of breezes
and hiding their beaks
in their feathers.

A small boy opened his window—
and spoke out loud.

If there were two witnesses,
would they distribute the seed
beneath my branches?

Would they weep in the night,
a bittersweet song,
would they disappear
with the morning light?

A pigeon, blue-grey,
died with a missing heart
among the wood boxes;
she had been cooing reticent
honours to the murmuring.

The pigeon boxes
collected straw.
Millet seed
dispersed over the ground,
and the birds flew in from the sky.

Only one was left dead when the girl
returned, softly singing.

A Street of Many Doors

There was a row of doors,
each different, speaking like the mouth of a house
as they opened and shut,
whereby the words could come in and go out.

There was the ornamental screen door on each,
white, brown, black, red, framing the entrance
while citizens of Mission City sat on their porches:
one old plaid woman in a rocking chair,
a young guy with long hair, strumming
his silver-stringed banjo.

Fleur was the little woman;
she stood at the gate to the garden at dusk,
the fragrance rose and cracked,
the petals were like the folds of her dress.
"We love our house," she said.
"Our house has deep shadows;
the shadows of saying hello
and the shadows of saying goodbye."

I climbed on my delivery bike with its basket
and rode through the street all night
with the downtown newspapers.
They were folded like origami.
By five, it was early morning,
and the sun was just beginning to rise.
I was standing in the street in ripped jeans;
it beheld my sackcloth as a fierce tiger lily.

A House of Many Walls

The tall Mission windows, where time and distance meet,
looked out over the populace passing by in the street;
I placed two glass lanterns with flues on two lamp stands.
Then I filled them with olive oil from Israel's last strands
echoing down the Mount of Olives.

The lamps burned through the day and into the night
lighting a lofty perch of dizzying height
where my wood ladder reached
almost to the ceiling roses and plaster cornices,
against the stacks of books in all languages, all colours,
and there were bookmarks emboldening the quotes
from the holly hedgerow.

She grows in orderly descant on Cemetery Road,
a tiny woman in green becomes this bed of thorns,
and renaissance from the inkwell flows
while the morning's dew each grave adorns.

There were thin walls in this old house of herbs,
the opaque cups filled with boiling water curbed
the taste for anything but tea: rich, deep, and smooth;
the doors opened when the flood of customers came through,
laughing in a myriad of colours, that they had found you.

Now the blue glass glows at even bright,
one tall pillar candle burns steadily—though the night,
the beeswax emits its character light in shallows dulcet,
burning the candle at both ends and two hemispheres met;
no one could accuse you in your coldness of going South.

When the winter comes, you'll be miles ahead
with the camomile for all those fallen ill in bed.

Emerging Sparrows and Salt

A sparrow flew out over the rooftops—
a small creature, unseen,
yet a small girl opened her window—
and wished the bird Godspeed.

If there were two bags of salt,
two witnesses,
now there are many—
in nascent culpability
to define good and evil
in the light of community.
The salt dispersed over the ice.

Wherever a sparrow emerges
and flies,
do we remember her still?

Portrait of a Young Girl

Her aunt gave her mother a bouquet of lilies when she was born.
Her ears were small and ivory, the shape of lily of the valley petals.
The doctor had sat up late burning the midnight candle.

That was how she was known:
burning the beeswax at both ends.
The flames of hope were higher.
Her long dark hair creased down her back.
Her eyes were as deep as the pools of night.
Her friends were fidelity.
They were old souls with bent wings who found
their solace in paradise
among the water lilies.

There was a memory of laughter;
it was the humour that kept her straight-backed
even though she had scoliosis.
Sometimes the pain made her mute and
tears ran out the sides of her eyes.
Her mother had always dreamed she would play the piano,
but an hour a day was some form of torture.
She called it her torturous chair.
Even as a child, her small hands
wrapped around the edges
of the wood upholstered seat. And still she said nothing.
She could hang upside down off the seat.
Her mind could walk on the ceiling.
It made sense to her to see everything upside down.
The metronome would tick calmly in the room.
She would write down notes of a scale:

semitone, tone, tone in pencil.

When she was older,
there were suitors who sat up as straight as she did;
They sat across from each other
and stared each other down
until tears ran out of the sides of her eyes.
The stipulations around her
were as granite grey as a pirate's rock,
and they were unsure whether she was a sunken treasure.

The ancient sea
lapped the shore. There was only
the light on the horizon now.

For a Dying Crown

Wreathed in eucalyptus and sitting
at the window, she is Euphrates divided
in two. There is the Queen's Wood
and the castle; here is the rabbits' lair,
there is the maiden's hair.
The silence endows the trees,
the amber is thick with moss,
and fog hangs midair.

One commentator,
and one orator—
the media is a fight to the death.
I must not give up. My sword is clean.
With every breath my last, I pledge
to defend my country. This country is
my soul, the very breath of it my essence:
the once stagnant aura of mediocrity
has shape-shifted into an oracle of power.
The very circle gives off its energy,
the vapours and perfumes of a former time
are deeply rooted in Jewish lore.

There is one station I meet
the requirement of: one diploma
that has been given me: one oil.
Lest I not carry it out
there is a sentence on Siberian Fir.
The death cult will
take you down with them.

There is a new hierarchy here:
the one with the most gifts is at the top,
the one who receives the most packages
has power.
A white thunder through the door
is concussive.
I wish I had said in a
percussive way, "I won't buy."

The Blouse

There are shell buttons
on the delicate front,
the lace collar
and almost eyelet
dreams in cream
from a retro boutique

with a reed
in New York City
vibrating
in a space as dark as an oboe.

The street song
beside an instrument case
with a faded velvet
interior
still innocent,
not mother-stained,
and accomplished
in the same moment:

there is a window
in this space.
There is a lick.

Footnote: In popular music genres such as country, blues, jazz or rock music, a lick is "a stock pattern or phrase" consisting of a short series of notes used in solos and melodic lines and accompaniment. For musicians, learning a lick is usually a form of imitation (Source: Wikepedia).

The Mahogany

Her high heels clicked
on the marble floor.
The diamonds in her ring
sparkled like they had been rinsed
with Dove.
This is it:
"You've arrived."
They stared out over
the city.
They were both brunettes.

I am glass,
I am a tower,
and the tallest,
rising 26 floors
in the city in the country.

Eyes clear, blink, blink,
a Picasso.
Into the sky it roams;
a girl in a black bonnet
with a stork wielded over
its frame in the moonlight.
Cinderella in the street
raised her head—
a salute.

Clay Hearts

A Catholic Star

In this dim light under a distant star,
there was a fortune to amass from bravery,
where colour distorts, exhales, and could now mar—
this people groaning 'neath the yoke of iron slavery.

Stirring my memory, bright they came:
people of heaven, not of men or same
as the desperately poor or reaching wretched,
we asked for alms from their anointed heads.

The Catholics would cast away with ease
all manner of hunger, sickness and disease,
they would stretch out a hand to your brood
of young, too many mouths and not enough food.

O joy, to receive from the higher realms:
when growing old with cares, bringing cloth bags,
my tattered highland clothing now in rags,
the crushed flowers of our souls, already used film.

This country was not endorsing hunger nor suffering
for those who had forgotten sin and mirrors.
The path to a cared-for life was not so clear;
there was an imbalance in the skies for the hurting.

The rain began to pour when they were sad,
the sun would shine its light when they were glad,
what momentary whispers of the wind's cold
would shake the poplar's gold.

Hark! My friends who stand at the gate of fear,
there is no hunger and no poverty here,
this is a refuge for your tired bodies now,
you can see the way through winter's snowy bow.

A blizzard had stopped us and we turned back,
but now we pressed forward into the black.
The future is unlike a stone olive press,
press on, and bottled at its best.

Midnight in the Street

My hands are blackened and dry,
my throat can only sing like a nightingale,
the asphalt street is quiet and stale,
so the song rings like a man's cry.

They usually say, are you a thief in the night?
Or a witch in flight?
Why does the baser world
reward you with its continuity?
Leaves swirled around the autumn
of my crystal sight,
the mist, like a death dance, twirled.

Where does my wealth accrue:
whom does the star on the horizon represent
in jewelled sparks—
the North star is lonely and dark,
she is supernal with visions,
not the medicine of pain,
nor the moon with its lesions,
this woman to evil cannot consent,
she stands alone too.

When her face is streaked with tears,
the sky lonely rains, as seers
prophesy the weather;
they are beyond your brothers,
they pick up women on street corners
only to return them to their brothel fears,
but they are what's bold and bright—
in this time beyond the sunlight.

When you can't even hear the sound
of the owl's feather,
yet it floats to earth, untethered
from the streetlight perch;
this is an underground church—
when the wind is famous and wild,
and you are its child,
somewhere loved and found.

Don't cry anymore,
don't let down your hair to the floor.

The Weeping Branch

O country of sweet sheaves, hear my humble invitation;
the branches are weeping.
There has been a struggle in the baser realms,
the virtue of the earth has been shaken.
I bring with me the spirit of Canada,
a pleading to your noble station.

The world has seen your heart despised.
I spoke to you and you replied.
When I sing of revolution in the dead of night,
you hear.
Then answer me with all your might.

This is the moment of the turning,
and it is not for the weak;
much is at stake.
I prophesied the sanguine salt was guileless,
and chunks of coal were your revenge in darkness.
The oyster sun spoke over the sea,
churning the machinery of democracy.

O Canada:
I was born into the quiet moments of Windsor,
I am a prophet under the order of Samuel.
Canada's gates will never be shut;
I am last to call my people home.
I am in it 'till the bitter end.

Dogwood Manor

Dogwood Crest

Lulla-lu, there is a voice here.
Lullaby-lu, a child sighing,
the wind is crying,
the fairies hide, dear.

Lulla-lu tiny child,
you open your small hands,
your eyes are wider to lands.
Lullaby-lu, slumber mild.

Your basket swings under the dogwood tree,
the flowers open to cradle the new,
and beloved generations before you,
their fragrance encircles me.

You are a lamb in the peppermint,
wooly-girl, a docent to the gallery
of books, in a field encircled by trees,
the grass and herb leaves glint.

All are loved within this circle of trees,
sanctity is royal navy,
and marriage is fit for a lady,
redeemed to loyalties.

Lulla-lu, but rest in sleep,
now off to the lullaby world
said your mother's curls,
before the shadows creep,
before the branches weep.

Spiritual Touch

The touch of a king
would condescend to heal;
if one was touched
one hundred times,
one would turn into a princess.

If you had loved
so dearly, the beloved:
the early sky, a dark jewel
in domes of foreign temples.

Their hands clasped,
knees tightly bent,
a burning sword
thrust between
the mind and soul;
and the deepened heart
will arise in the splendour
of modesty.

One million children
stand at the gates
of their straw village,
asking to be let through:
to where the golden bird
welcomes dawn,
the translucent orb of sun-star
crossing the sky
from morning to sunset;
I tend my mantra of gardens
just before dusk…

The glass of time, so fragile,
and cloven antelope hooves
upon the sand:
tidings meant to clothe despair with
purity, the oils of acacia
and eucalyptus.

Glassy water
in the riverbed, too dry;
the speaking of the white raven,
and unheard silence:
my memorized word
so clear and vibrant—
to a diseased room.

What enchantment
shall I break to heal you?
O ebony soul, caught within
the prisons of deformity
and the sepulchre
of infertility and pain:
Peace.

The kiss of wisdom
is a touch piece,
and the dying,
healed do ascend.

A New Valley

While I was waiting here,
he conducted the symphony:
his head was wreathed in clouds,
he had climbed a mountain
and the air was thin, but there
was a message for him at the top.

He spoke of new beginnings,
a time for children to be born,
to be rosy-cheeked with health;
a time to plant the fields,
a time for new ideas,
and countries to be made over.

I bought a lavender farm:
its fragrance rolled off into the sunset,
I was emaciated
with reckoning, afraid to live
and unprepared to die,
unsure how to continue.

This is a new vein—
being extravagant, healing souls
with rough flowers,
gathering the bitters in linen,
now that the fear is over,
when we reach a summit
and dare not go on alone.

Holding hands is new oil
that flows through the valley
of San Jacinto,
where I dream and you speak:
the oratorio glistens with wealth—
of thoughts and revelation.

Time for a Woman Poet

I would be born a poet in a coat,
I keep this letter to you in my pocket, casting
you, I will give it to you in time lasting,
although I would rather milk the goat.
I've lived a thousand years, in league with tea,
I drink in more and more of earth's light,
with every cup, I sanction blight;
a woman who informs with words the trees.

For no one holds my hand upon the road,
I walk forever with no observant end,
am I expecting strangers or friends around the bend?
and heavy-lidded is the horse's load.
He plods with cares I could not comprehend,
even and staid, I hold his mane,
he eats his oats and keeps me sane,
a horse's nature I would recommend.

There is a hill I lingered on,
fast as the light was fading low,
the moon had almost risen through night's blow,
into the future I gazed long.
A creator could not lie beneath the ground,
she would fly away—a solemn bird,
or insist years later on being heard,
her voice would, as seas, unrelentless pound.

Her old thick voice would be an ancient roar
of blood beneath the ground that fed the roots
of heavy trees with their dusky fruit,
grapes would cry at winepress upon the floor.
It became a red wine river flowing down
to an oil sea, where I found a hand
extended as a moon shines o'er the land,
illuminating the first peoples' indigo crown.

It was then I could see future's subtle shape,
a rabbit disappeared into its glen,
a deer within the meadow nibbling then,
I could affix my broken wing with tape.
But slowly I die as the world peaks,
my essence ebbs away, a shrinking empire:
the verse that once sang as a carefree lyre
is now the hardwood floor that creaks.

My chest of treasures holds
mementoes of me pausing blue,
the shape-shifting need for the spirit mood
to live in a vase or some other mould.
As life bore down on me in myths,
the deepening of each ponderous basin,
the cracking of porcelain's pandemonium,
became doctors condemning wordsmiths:

They could not die, or they would rise,
they could not live, for faintness exclusive,
they breathe last breaths, hiding reclusive,
they could not pray, it would be lies.
Thus the smoke rises early and remotely,
preparing me for another day of praise,
of the war within that makes me raise
worship to its feet shyly:

It was a dead friend in a tomb sealed,
he had lain there many days as old hymns,
and now no one had eyes weeping anymore, rims
of sunken sight, when they could be healed:
I stretched out my hand,
I called our broken worship to come forth—
where we all criticised our brethren's worth,
and made him sweat and till the land.

Levites, I will be a singer if there is a song,
while wringing the last of the water
from the linens, I hum at bees' laughter,
a woman is a word-keeper all the day long.
The convent is not too far south
of this old house in the back-woods of Mission—
they might be associates of rites and confessions,
and contemplation did not need a mouth.

This Is Where You Keep Me

I.
If I did not die young,
I would become baroque
in movement,
and emotional relevance.
I climbed a hallmark tree
within a child,
I bade her try her pen,
and not be wild as the sea.
The rolling island hills
remind me of England's
pleasant green.
The fort is aged and
crumbling, now a relic
in the sun glinting offshore.
There was one thing I
wanted to tell you:
I have written it down
on this folded piece of lined paper.
Life has not become
a busload of people,
rather eclectic,
that I don't know and haven't met.
Of course, I was
on my way to music lessons,
the cool dark interior
of a house in Oak Bay.
I would play for my
medieval teacher
something she had not heard.

II.
I have seen you all your life,
but I had not heard you before,
I did not know that you
could play with anger,
and I would notice.
You are without malice,
an African violet;
I am only a mother
and I do not have time.
Write your lessons,
and your teachers will be proud
that you are obedient,
young and strong.
Do you know where
I want you to end up:
I want you to have tea
with me when you're four
and when you're forty.
We are a tea-party of two,
and if books abound,
there is no need to write.
Just listen:
listen to the singing,
listen to the eventide's note,
the disappearing light,
and the last flown
yellow-rumped warbler.

III.
My teacher stoked the fire
of my mind,
as the flaming red curls
to her waist.
Her voice was like
Fitzgerald in the Jazz Age,
and it was liquor.
The piano was
black and smooth
beneath my touch,
inviting a cadence.
There was a woven tapestry
in the room, and it lent
acclaim to a regal woman
with a long line of students.
To try any new music,
I would have her approval
and in the era
the arts would communicate
involvement.
I wanted the church's approval
to write, but I did not ask,
or I might not have completed
a long list of things to do.
There are gate-keepers
of our inner children,
so I only asked to play
inside the black wrought-iron gate:
this is where you keep me.

IV.
You are beloved and
this is where you keep me,
I am a photo
in a locket over your heart.
I am your mother:
on summer days
you gather your picnic
with wildflowers,
and take a blanket.
It was my golden
rag-time piano that could
turn a tune,
reminding you of the roaring twenties.
This was a proper house.
I was a minister's wife,
wore a dress,
and baked pies.
There was homemade bread
from the grain
I ground,
and kept in the cold storage.
Why do I have to ensure
you are good enough
to write,
and take what comes as
a result?
You are old enough
with your pen to make your
own decisions,
somehow you'll survive
behind your own black gate.

V.
I might be only
an aspen sapling,
or I might be old now,
with glittering leaves,
and porous bones, who is to say?
The tea from long ago
is still steeping in my cup.
The dance of time
continues on,
and little girls join
with new pink shoes.
I sat at the window
for a few years,
wondering if it was a feast
or a famine.
I joined the army
and they made me head up
the Canadian military
with pomp and gunfire.
They still stand at attention,
waiting for me to be born,
while hailing in unison
a new world.
This is the Baroque period
if we have our own opinions
on corsages, buns, and bobby pins
and how it should be done with grace.
We are married again,
the reverence sounded,
we are irregular jewels.

A History of Temperance

Historical Hurricane

The recession stretched for almost a decade,
as vast rooms that go on and on,
as the lucid dreams
over oak floors
temper the alpine mist.

The flamenco-red walls,
and the kaleidoscope of lights
endeared history.
Here I sit—
bold and proud as
a tartan plaid.

I could dance in an organic whole
of limbs and pauses
before the hurricane;
with a rather moody folk skirt
brushing the granite hearth.

There was only a wind at the chimney.

That would be my signature style
of delicate arches,
brilliant height,
and stony-blue curves.

What the Lilac Was Not

The lilac was not lustrous,
but rather historic,
alas, I did have to explain
each delicate trivet of colour,
each satin sheen of purple,
next to the rich plum and deep wood.

The flourishing variety of botanicals
beyond the velvet drapery,
through the meld of glass,
echoed its mystery,
a contrast to the century-old moulded
plaster ceilings,
growing archaic with beauty.

Simply, the garden
unfolded through time
like a linen cloth,
with each dried flower held
in it as potpourri.

A Little Fury

It was a magical silver wood,
all glittering with the dew,
where the light gleams through morning's seams,
and fairy wings are not lack-luster,
speaking of iridescent things.

A furious thunder storm sprang up, threat-laden
from the other end of the garden,
where the hummingbirds and bumblebees
hang on florets, like tea bags in steeping tea,
sipping the drifting transient fragrance
before darting into the forest oak trees
that are solid before the fury.
The grey squirrels and the rabbits scurried,
even their young were hurried
into their burrows before the wind.

The storm haphazardly whipped
the evergreen branches root to tip,
scattering fern fronds hither and thither;
the aristocratic deer will not today delay,
though they usually in these paths meander,
drinking the nectar from flowers of clover.
The rain melted the blue and green
into rivulets pristine.

In Relevant Cards

Feeling lost in the room
of hickory-plated emotions,
where dreams could be almost trite,
there were deep roots and tall branches
of the tree of my life,
that brushed my skin
when I stopped in the card aisle.

I am too innocent
to consider that my most jaded sentiments
could be passable in a card, leisurely and soft,
with underwriters,
hope under their belts.

My anger melts like ice cream,
sweet and sticky, with chocolate chips,
drips to be caught as holidays and moments
when we can't forget to send
a wish, a note, a card…

Petrified Wood

There is something durable
about immortality,
the iconic style of nature—
a petite woman
in a little black dress.
She is first living and warm,
then aging:
turning from sepia browned,
to diamond-icy and dying,
then dead with journalistic starkness.

And she rises
each spring,
with her immortal cloak
of colour. Dazzling gardens,
a glitz of fragrance,
shooting the crystalline rain
clear through
with sun,
bereft of fear
of her time in arrears.

Apples of Gold in Settings of Silver

When you spoke, I listened,
and it was as the pattering of rain
after a long dry spell in the Fraser Valley,
soaking the yellow ground.
There were diamonds of glassy water
like tears on the eyes
of the flat blueberry fields.
They welled up
into juicy night-blue stones,
like sapphires grow in caves
for Lady Sappho.

The baby, in her white eyelet bonnet,
sat on a blanket in the afternoon.
She was the muse of time
and the canyons of her ears
heard the songs of the rivers and the forests;
we painted her that day
on cardboard,
as we could not afford a canvas.

Reservoir Blue

The potter's wheel turned around and around,
lassitude becoming pottery
from deep within the ground.
Clay being tamed and pulled
from a wild blue coal:
fierce and swift, to re-worked, reserved,
light over the sea, conserved.

This sentimental moulding is making you resent
being rather old-fashioned,
the subtle blue glaze to wet rock rationed.
It was traditional that you take a deep dive
into colour's blood,
there were the jewel tones, rather serene linens,
hanging stars in a dark wood.

I am of beauty and all she holds captive,
you said—
must I explain this prolific art
of turning 'round and 'round as a thousand earths.

Breathing Space

Where the robin red-breast made its nest,
there was a sweeping fence
overhung with subtle evergreen trees
beside the timeless garden of cornstalks,
spindles of beans,
and square strawberry leaves.

Here, in heaven
there is a window to our little earth,
where, peering through the glass
we see quite clearly—
The old steeple bells ring with song
to the purple ground
and the royalty of the wood—
this artist's green
subdued the spider's finite threads
with a crack of rain chenille.
Then the layered reparation
of old and new,
like oldest leaf clung
to newest bloom.

View of Mount Song

Did love the 'morrow break,
when winter came too fast to me,
and seeped under the door,
a mist rose o'er the woolen floor,
too fast held tightly to my feet,
and bound them.

All weighing in my despair,
I lost my soulful child there,
all hurried in the straw street.
The wind passed by
the ashen flower box and swept it nigh,
camellias to a fiery finish.

What of comfort here in the Orient,
a far away land of copper hands and lotus flowers.
A wall surrounds my heart, my days
have all been lost in a maze
of rice fields, cries ringing out from dawn, I sing
only in the dark amid burning embers on the lawn.

I am far away, too hot to touch, too alone to stay.
The sun is a round red circle in white sky.
My books are scattered in a nomad pile.
I wrote to you in burnt sienna style.

I am neither poor nor rich.
I am neither young nor old.
I am neither black nor white.
I am neither slave nor free.

In the Custody of Angels

I stood here for quite some time
with my back to you,
I was an ancient sky
decorated with only the sunrise,
and the smoke curled from the chimney
rather like the curls on your neck.

I took my angel wings and rose
from the place of a wood stove,
a fire table, and a poet
in a cabin by the river.
The clouds reflected my appearance
and equivocal disappearance.

Once I knew you quite well
and I thought you would never leave me.
I only know now that if you fly away
I'll fly away too:
the nocturne thrush twittered
on a branch just outside the clematis fence.

Beyond your prison you could see the sky
of my custodian.
You are in the custody of an angel.
She is bright, flashing and you
water-coloured her world—
just so from aged.

Recession Icons

Beside the Golden Door

"Give me your tired, your poor,
your huddled masses yearning to breathe free,
The wretched refuse of your teeming shore,
Send these, the homeless, tempest-tossed, to me:
I lift my lamp beside the golden door."
— Emma Lazarus, 1883

I had not been afraid of the dark for a long time now.
My father was once scrambling eggs in bacon grease;
life was not for the faint. Everything becomes ashes.
It's not a real job unless you get your hands dirty . . .

This all started back during the recession in Canada,
a time something like the Great Depression.
People could not even afford to feed their children
and they would send them to school hungry.
Drive until you can drive no more…

To even turn away a glass of milk
was considered ungrateful.
You said thank you to God at every meal.
Your eyes are wide open.
You can't do this job and be soft…

Rival, you stopped telling fairy tales for once
and admitted you were short on dimes—
that is why you stand in the street.
You are singing, though, a song in time gone by.
Stand, until your bones ache with exhaustion…
Brother, can you spare a dime?

The Little Match Girl

In the dark, a little girl in a cotton shawl
struck a match to keep warm.
It illumined the stone structure
of the Peace Tower she leaned against,
the gargoyles against the night sky.
Gothic architecture
reaching almost to heaven
stretched its lacy fingers,
blotting the stars with its handkerchief—
its rhetorical icons
simmering prayers in the shadows.

There was a patchwork quilt
of nations, that had grown faded
with the rain and snow,
of the many colours of skin
that made up the face of a country,
of the many films from the National Film Board.

A match box was ten cents;
a passerby gave her a dime
as she stood in the gutter,
and she collected them in her apron.

A Second June

Survivalist, how deep is the wound?
There is a second sun, a second June,
disparate over the terrace
where golfers play seraphs
after the first iced-tea afternoon.

This is the letter to my second wind,
where I rename myself Canadian;
eloquent islanders travel the roads within,
and paint the world by re-framing.

Poverty causes angst among martyrs,
among the once wealthy—
selling the rings of their former partners,
what people will do for money.

What people will do out of desperation
tells something of their ruffled character feathers,
and newspapers have absconded restoration—
they have fallen on hard times and rainy weather.

A Third April

The third time the spring came in
she wore Laura Ashley with hues of mint,
a dash of thyme, that friend of mine,
and a hat with a hint of velvet.

She hung a flower on the wood wall,
and many more irises appeared
in purple and orange, the brightest colour
under the ten commandments.
Moses would engrave
your name
in a leather-bound Bible.

What prophet would I ask
to interpret the recession
and the subsequent poverty:
Moses or Samuel?
The next door neighbour lost his job,
his daughter joined a homeless camp,
my grandmother's second husband died
of Coronavirus,
my father could not leave a tip,
while I bought even more irises than before.

Sky Wreath

Where the ivy tresses curl on the brick wall
beyond the cream sashes,
how do I remark of the browned landscape,
why would I reveal its bitter heritage—
a line of leafless maples—
its well of blood,
its bruised remnants, covered with snow,
its silvered pencil scratching for liberty...

And the minions of earth conceal
the frozen swans in black gloves
at season's wintry white,
the buoyant spice with cloven antlers
in heated ion discourse,
and why four apples and the tiny round cardamom
munitions swim darkly, hidden in the cider,
when the early indifferent smoke
from the chimney wreaths the sky.

Dreamscape Gray

Handsome, my sepulchral lot,
to lie within a churchyard plot,
to close my eyes in morbid air,
there is nothing I take with me there—
beneath the old ash tree.

My eyelids are now sealed forever,
no more to flutter—just encounter—
spirits of a better kind,
sojourned to my pallid mind.

I have died from sea to sea,
where I cried with morning's icy throng
and evening's tea.

There was a tear
that fell into my cup;
no more to handle,
I have lived enough.

My Little Black Book

In search of stones
to adorn the graves of those I have left behind—
it is true, you were once a friend,
now I can only mourn you
as a sweet wind mourns the pines,
for once you were very present in me,
and I could not forget your preferences
in music and in lunch, out-of-the-way haunts,
they were paramount to our keeping,
the bonding crafts that kept our hands busy.

I thought today, perhaps if I send you this note,
you will remember the good times we have had,
the griefs we have forgotten,
and take me out of the cupboard of your heart,
dust me off, and revive me.

Swan Drum

Sonnet of Tears

Along the Highway of Tears, far from home,
I was deep in my own heart as I hummed,
the cars in multicoloured rhythm drummed
a stretch of road so lonely I could roam.
Yet, one car stopped and would not pass me by,
he motioned too, with ulterior name,
then signalled me, a moth unto his flame,
avoiding the dark rain, I sat inside.
As sea birds fly into the bulwark's brine
waters, cresting ocean, I was caught up
by the notion I was saved—and by love,
we struggled at the next stop 'neath the pines.
A silenced mind, I was no longer free,
beaten, my heart, was resting on his knees.

Jacob's Ladder

Early in the morn, wee lassie, our sun
belongs only to us, as to new day:
the trees move on the cliffs with the wind, run—
gallop as the livery of thoughts stray.
There's a fair space where we spoke in burnished
freedom to tell the ancient firelight tales,
behold the minds of youth were once furnished
with reason and rhyme, cloaked with silver mail
of the righteous who walk to church to sing.
Now they've forgotten the song of the tree,
hills ache with silence where their hymns would ring
as a bell breaks solitude, mutiny.
Taxed, they will climb until they climb no more;
the Ladder of Jacob fell to the poor.

Salty Purse

That one low call of evening, stuttered breath,
arrested my thought and dragged it away:
more than moving rain symphonies in May,
wildflowers for the heads of women, wreathed,
children who would never tire and grow old
playing forever in the dusty street,
golden heads in a field of hard red wheat,
shivering by a heater in the cold,
reciting civil lines of English verse,
then hoping for the conscience's token piece,
but subsisting on the fare of crabmeat,
remnant of the blue ocean's salty purse.
Whatever we may tire of while the poor,
is now the indulgence of those with more.

Vintage Lamp

Observing a vintage lampshade in hand,
questioning the blue shadows and the light
that serenade the infant born in bright
starched fabric crib, the blurry tempest land—
the servant stands, beating the cooling palm.
The sculpture of the lamp's enamelled base,
athlete of all pertaining to the race
toward morning—the resistance's oily balm,
mother of this era, a busy throng
moving on, smoky denouement in form
telling of the path beneath my feet worn
to candles from the lamp of moonlit song.
Grassroots binding of the look from wasteful
to the cry for ancient things more tasteful.

Spikenard Madonna

When you stood in the brightened dawn of youth,
morning sun lit your head to searing flame,
the jewel that was your crown bore your name,
and sceptre bent authority to truth.
We were orphans, standing in your courtyard,
no bliss of parenthood to claim our fate,
no blimey kiss of death to stir our hate,
she took a bottle of ancient spikenard.
Madonna bore us, pouring out her oil;
she called us all her child in heart matters,
our minds, in retrospect, once wore tatters.
In gingham aprons we would cook and toil,
in the woods and fields, our hands would quick spy
what nature left, rust berries for the pie.

Cherry Trees in Blossom

Where the cherry trees touch dusk in descant—
wine branches blossom effulgent bright white,
all darkness of the time for this full night—
I wander 'neath the fading light, recant.
Seasons of my soul were like a grand home
I sojourned in once, for the staid calling
when all life pauses before the falling.
The invalid was destined to find none
of the aforementioned illness beneath
these eaves of healthy grandeur, sunlight near
the slant of shadows, refracted prism tear
that moved over the house, the sea, the heath.
If I, in fury, could my earth restrain,
I would—a hundred blossoms in my train.

Swan Song: From the Ashes of Plague

I lingered over the lake as swan song,
I was a mist, the garment that I drew
when I had no boundary to wings, flew
into the wind, and collected loud drawn
out images of clothing or shroud. Throngs
eyed my scarves in lama wool, and life brewed
its own garden vegetables, lamb, for stews.
I stopped. I, life, was stopped. Sweat at the gong
trickled down my alabaster face, dust—
marble dust, blown away by the master.
My Michelangelo and his sculpting
ceased to unnerve my patriotic cusp,
I was solid; I, the mass of stone cast,
I was iron and clay in one scything.

Swan Song: Echo

Echo, he said. The voices of flour sacks
reached higher on the treble clef, rising;
a utopia instead of a scream
erupted like dark on planet's backs.
There was a falling on the table, jacks
tumbled out of a little girl's fist, seams—
even berries, red threads of Levi's jeans.
Her earring collection was in a rack
in her jewellery box of green velvet,
she threaded blue and white marbled
beads on silver, and grew into a swan
from an ugly duckling, when the heat melted.
It was past giving Valentines, garbled
a new society in deep fawn.

Swan Song: Did the Pear Tree Survive?

This is the nicest dress you have ever
seen in moss-wind, blowing over the cliffs;
I am standing here, there are the lows, lifts,
and great moments—there is a sound, tremor
emanating from the mountain's side, lore
of dragons who have swallowed princesses.
The flakes of gold fell in drifts of snow, myths
two feet deep that melted, flood—more
vanquishing than all previous troubles,
crippling our deepest intentions at love,
making communion too intimate, wine
next to a poet, and winery next to bubbles
floating over the freshly mowed green, doves
on the pear tree that was wick back in time.

Swan Song: Fishing Boats

There was a silent moon. It had a hue
around it; over the sea the boats bobbed
in navy waters, and the light house throbbed
its sonorous pulse, resonant and true.
The ocean was in mist, carded grey-blue—
the yarn of a former time, women sobbed
only behind closed doors, as men went off
to sea. All who were sailors; both genders grew
pale at the task of fighting viral load
in invisible sea monsters everywhere.
As their sense of their sea legs sore increased,
they became more curt, sea captains bloated
with disinfectant, pride in dinnerware—
long tables presided, lilacs, depressed.

Swan Song: Water the Driftwood Flowers

Let's begin again: all society
sound now. Throes of music are upon us;
we must resist, we must desist. We must
do nothing, we do things in piety.
Only now this came about: deity
of a plague, we must hear. You too are us.
We are all the same. We are viral lust.
We will love and mate, or we will kill three.
How now do you propose to indict us
with greater powers over life and death?
If you offer us our own fate, how could
we refuse? We pull our hooded capes up
over our bowed heads. Now our very breath
condemns us, as partners in crime (beachwood).

Swan Song: A Silver Sunrise

My feet were strewn with kelp on the seashore.
I watched and waited for you to come home.
The sun red rose and set in silver stone.
The setting was only what brought out more
garnet gem-like specs of your secret store.
Dark hair down her back, girl with a salt moan;
she has disappeared from view 'neath pinecones,
beneath the piles of bleached-pale apple cores.
Her face was decisive, she was not dew;
perhaps she would be happy elsewhere.
She was the jewel in the Jeweller's crown;
you worked long hours for this one ewe.
As lonely ones admit their seaward cares,
some did not admit their fear they would drown.

Swan Song: Once Upon A Time

The drifts snow-white cover my apple hair,
I have been poisoned by a fairy tale,
the skeleton of a handsome tail;
there were vile warnings not to eat this fare,
on the tapestried green maternal chair.
The fine chocolate was dark and nightly veiled,
as a Persian queen of an empire mailed
her subjects with gossamer notions, chaired
her conscience by a board of designs
both ornate and established, elegant.
She kissed the Prince who turned into a frog:
he leapt, he groaned, he then his past resigned,
the worth of his life's brow, maleficent…
and hopped away to an imperial bog.

Goose Wing by Moon

I nestled my beak in my taupe feathers,
the moon had almost risen; it was night.
The waters of Fish Trap Creek shone their bright
hue in the solstice of crisp blue winter,
the essence of the earth was as ether.
Once under the sun, now the dark's night-light
shone cream resplendent, oval and lips tight.
Gathering, reeds still in our beaks bitter,
I padded with my webbed feet into grass
that held me like a bassinet holds child,
my maternal breast both heavy and near.
I'd glided silently through water glass,
my wing was thought as proud as I was mild,
my presence was not damp nor fraught with fear.

Goose Wing by Night

When night fell over the nature reserve
our wings fluttered, fell, with the murky dark,
where we waited in our gaggle with stark
memory of the way we were preserved.
There was an aspen tree, leaning reserved—
and it was the scratched home of a blue lark—
pandemic sang that we would be sin-marked.
The bird song rings, we listened in, conserved.
Could there come such dulcet sweet furious
mud? We would put our righteousness away,
and don worn clothes, to walk about in torn
linen. We walked on water as curios,
we turned cinnamon into curry in a day
when no more miracles occurred but morn.

Sonnet Potpourri

The light shone out a little bleary-eyed,
from every casement window to the night,
it was the little house that glimmered bright,
we walked the lake road to the water's side.
It was the home that we had waited for,
it spoke to us of hearth and firelight,
the attic rooms kept children within sight,
the plans we had would make us long for more.
Beneath the eaves the memories were dear,
and countless others had this way come by,
with dreams romantic, lovers that would tie
their hearts unto each other, ever near.
We counted every penny with intent,
but came up short, with modest discontent.

When I have lived my years, I shall recall
of days when I would not recant my youth,
the hours I walked among the sandy dunes,
observing gulls that flew 'till they were small
upon horizons far 'neath dusty moon.
My mother was the sea, my father, sun—
I was the morning light through seaweed dun,
that tides had strung the shore we walked so soon.
If anything in childhood I regret,
my life would be too sentimental now,
when auburn frames an alabaster brow,
the names of all my starfish I'd forget.
What word I spoke in child-like melody,
became the verse that echoed from the sea.

When I would give my parting glance to thee,
when I would bid thee my austere good bye—
I give you my respect with lowered eyes—
passing by you, I would imagine me
with you, a better heaven than before.
I saw you rise to glory without qualm,
the storms of life had all resolved to calm.
Your aging rage had crashed upon the shore
as you conceded life was not to be
forever and forever of thy breath,
but families continue on into the next
years, and generations rise to thank thee.
When I would pay my last respects, in laud,
we all would give your well-deserved applause.

City of flowers, sweet moments at will,
remember me lonely as a kindness,
a sea-sick isle swept with reminiscence,
from starry wood-fenced meadow to the hill.
I played beneath the poplar trees at school,
a delicate child with gold braided hair:
I was your poet, knelt, composing there,
pupil of the largest transcendent pool.
Your children, Thetis and Saltspring, come by
for tea in a garden of fine incense,
steaming rose hips and lingering reasons
for conversing with a true butterfly:
sending you their translucent wing letters,
setting your thoughts free from iron fetters.

Lovely, my lovely when the night has passed,
I dream, though waking, my tears on your face,
I have lived my lifetime, and now your grace
has wakened me once more to autumn's last:
the leaves all turning as a crimson tide
vacating Dallas Point becomes the fall,
the moments before winter's silent call,
and the last mother stone cathedral's chide.
Her bells have rung out in the Sunday morn,
the whitened light through stained glass, glowing peers,
and falling snow will wait 'till late next year,
'till after the new dairy calves are born.
Fortuitous that I have heard you call,
before the ground is frozen, shadows tall.

Soldier-like, bravest man a rising moon—
backs to earth—there is a war—they'd open
their eyes, if on their eyes they could depend,
before all loyal sons lie in their tombs.
Hills, look to the hills—who'll join me, not one?
No longer have I a friend to think of,
all my patriot friends are fallen doves.
No one thinks better than of his own son,
a mother's tear would not forget this morn—
for here I stand, a lonely soldier last.
Fly from me enemy! Fly from my past!
I have courage for war until I'm torn,
and it is fully time, fly from me then.
Undeceive thyself from my contagion.

Now to my end I come in stately black,
for I am but a prisoner of this earth,
I can't escape its clutches or its wrath,
nor any of its loves, nor laughs, nor births.
I bear the lovely France a final fleur,
I witness of this hour before the flame,
for all my visions have been of one cœur—
I cry to God, unyielding of his name.
Do not my hands untie, lest I recant—
for I am but a bird that cannot fly.
Do not relent, for I shall not repent;
my sweetest fame is written now on high.
You look upon my pure and martyred face,
that in the flame of love has found its grace.

If I have loved you in my silent ways,
I have stayed at home with thoughts a-cower.
I have made a mincemeat pie with white flour,
my heart is growing anxious with each day.
I would but buy the barley, shuck the corn,
if my old life was worth one penny jar,
if I restored the sear of every scar,
now boisterous ideas would be scorned.
One thousand bills ran to my velvet door,
there was no money to repay my debts,
before my creditors called for my rent,
each phone call ringing louder than before.
I'll laugh again before my death is o'er,
because you were my crimson desert flow'r.

Your last word in this pallid hospice realm
was miniscule as round millet is small,
impossible to catch beyond the hall,
yet indicative of golden ship's helm,
voyage looming onward into heaven,
far beyond this one sombre meaning filled
room, fragrant with flowers on the white sill,
from each child beneath your heart, all seven.
In righteous clothing you are finely dressed,
there was a call to you once with meaning,
past the world's inebriated dreaming;
what word of praise to give the very blessed?
The last moment with you I saw a door
you opened to the sick, the homeless, poor.

O flame that circles me—O wisdom's light,
seeking the way through my utter darkness,
hurtling from the outside through the starkness
to the inside of my heart, a dark night
of the soul cannot distance purer thee—
for I would write in ink your mind untold,
and fashion you as from clay to the world,
until the blind could endless, boundless see.
Through obsession I would find my novice;
she would be of one love and one desire,
lone in a convent cell she would retire.
She is blessed olive without one vice,
of a still-chaste, and contemplative place—
now humans could not boast to see this face.

Oblique Doors

Dimes

Multicoloured Maize

I can work for dimes,
I am as swift as a centaur
with a bow; I can read the skies—
I know when it will rain or snow.

Blue Maize

I will ride through the streets
before dawn,
and drop newspapers before people awake,
at their oblique doors.

Maple Tree Angel

I lift the curse over you
of blistered feet and bruised shins,
of the tiredness that makes women fall
down in a dead faint.

Newsprint

Multicoloured Maize

Whatever you print,
I will run with it,
declaring the facts are before you
to all newsprint readers.

Blue Maize

It will be a decade
before I tire of being first;
a messenger before the morning's
commencement.

Maple Tree Angel

I lift the curse over you
of being driven by fear,
that whatever is asked of you
you must comply without question.

Small and Shy

Multicoloured Maize

Who created the sky?
It is small and shy
at first light,
then later brilliant.

Blue Maize

There is no breathing space
without you;
you are the breath I breathe
mile upon mile.

Maple Tree Angel

I lift the curse over you
of a life like an athlete,
who pushes their body and their pain
to the limit of their endurance.

Rugged

Multicoloured Maize

The rain and the snow
cannot stop my engine
from running continually
all night, rugged over the rock salt.

Blue Maize

I am in and out of shadows,
feeling the rough bark of tree branches
with the moon my only companion.
I will not forget your love.

Maple Tree Angel

I lift the curse over you
of a life in the dark,
of blinds drawn,
and the fear of light.

One Minute Per House

Multicoloured Maize

I drive myself on, through the night,
with only one minute per house,
remembering that to be meaningful
I need only breathe pure prayer.

Blue Maize

The media is driven,
and relentlessly new each day,
but the stories are gritty
and full of the harshness of real life.

Maple Tree Angel

I lift the curse over you
of the unrelenting menial nature
of hard work,
and of a heavy yoke.

Early Light

Multicoloured Maize

Walk with me a few paces;
see how the mountains reveal their glory.
The early light drenched them, over
my numb fingers and hypothermic toes.

Blue Maize

A young man calls after me,
his name is Michelangelo.
He painted the sky by hand,
and sculpted each cloud; remember his name.

Maple Tree Angel

I lift the curse over you
of feeling like your goals as an artist
are just out of reach,
somewhere with the paint and brushes.

Wages

Multicoloured Maize

Break up the ground for the gourds
corn, and beans beneath the evergreen;
we will eat the Three Sisters, come fall
like chiefs at the harvest.

Blue Maize

If I wished to buy a loaf of bread
from my wages of twenty cents a house,
I would have to go to twenty-five houses.
I might think, why bother to eat bread?

Maple Tree Angel

I lift the curse over you
of the high cost of living,
of having to skip meals and go hungry
to make ends meet.

Mundane

Multicoloured Maize

My fear of the mundane
has made me travel at the speed of light,
in the twinkling of an eye, with nerves of steel,
undaunted by normal folk.

Blue Maize

I am saving desperate women
on street corners,
alerting endangered victims to foul play,
playing a threatening dame in back alleys.

Maple Tree Angel

I lift the curse over you
that you will go under for giving
a kind word to the homeless still straggling
in the street with their blankets, come morning.

Misfit

Multicoloured Maize

I am part of a new group
of nameless, faceless people,
a usually invisible family of misfits,
a cog in the machine.

Blue Maize

I don't ever quit, even in the hot sun,
even if it pours sheets of rain in the autumn,
even if I fall in the winter;
I am your witness, with a bird's eye view.

Maple Tree Angel

I lift the curse over you
from rising in the dead of night
to carry out a long arduous task
that on some days seems occult.

News Copy

Multicoloured Maize

I wake up in the dark,
and hit the floor running;
I will carry out today
all God's asking me to do.

Blue Maize

I will be the first
to receive the news copy,
I will be the first to hear
and then run with it for hours.

Maple Tree Angel

I lift the curse over you
from travelling into the land of the dead.
The one provision given to us
was enough for the journey.

Olive Oil

Multicoloured Maize

I light my lamp,
I remember to pray:
the olive oil will never run out,
the cistern will not run dry.

Blue Maize

The symbol of my commitment
to purity are the white garments
that have never been worn,
the cream cloths that have never been torn.

Maple Tree Angel

I lift the curse over you
of seven years of slavery
that represents our slavery to sin.
There was a coin in their mouth.

Oil of Heaven

Call to the Poets (Fantasia)

Where are the poets?
Where are their deep sonorous voices,
their caves hidden far within mountains?

Poets, I call you.

Where do they cry so no one hears,
espousing the distance
between God and humanity?

Poets I call you by darkness,
I call you by light.

Their burning embers are the eyes
that can see,
unblinded by night.

Poets, I call you by
your multi-faceted names,
your dominions,
your many lives in former places.

You and your spoken word
work their way into
the sands of our minds
as the sea—our castles

demolished each day
and washed away
into Solomon's tomb,
where his wives glow with aqua stones.

If a poet would speak,
the poem would live
in our shallow heartbeats, in the deep
trenches of our borders.

Monarch in the Subway (Da capo aria)

If I was reading,
I could be pouring over
any number of the two million
items put out that day:
as factual news article,
a joke, a myth,
a flinty poem,
a journal by someone
more innocent than I,
a novel about partners
I don't have.

If I was dancing,
nothing would sway me
(like a sway back)
deterring me from the barre,
closing my eyes
to Swan Lake in leotard.

If I had a camera,
in black and white, my dextrous fingers
would uncoil, strand by strand—
and, a passenger
in the subway,
I would lift my eyes
to notice a monarch butterfly
with cloudy wings,
parched,
dying on the sidewalk.

How can I capture you;
I can only
offend you with a lens,
and phone the metropolitan
to offer them your beauty's sleep.

I Heard the Owl Call My Name (Pasticcio)

The owl that you hear
two-hoots
so loud,
calling me,
that it echoes through
the whole town
of Stratford-upon–Avon—he flies
when all are asleep.

While he flies,
no one ever gets sick,
no one is tired
or sorry they were born,
has a face in a frown,
or walks upstairs and down,
all alone and forlorn,
when all are asleep.

The owl flies outside society,
his breath you will not see;
he is hidden deep
inside the bracken inside me,
saving his charges from leers,
brushing the grasses as spears,
eloping with the night wind's sound
when all are asleep.

A Patient Moment (Cabaletta)

I, the invalid,
am in good company
with a maze of sparkling hallways,
a hundred sterile hospitals,
beady-eyed doctors
with good bedside manners,
a host of diseases
to occupy my chart,
and nurses in a platoon,
their dozen thermometers
with or without mercury.

Do I want a life
with or without charity?
With or without
the poison,
dripping from the ceiling?
Formal or casual?
With or without
the trouble?
Ironed or wrinkled?
or somewhere in between.

Still Learning You (Verismo)

There is a curtain between us;
it has been there for ages,
and I have a Jewish priest
with a rope around his foot.
Unless he dies, he'll
be here with a word for you.

There is a calm upon
the stage with purposed eyes,
the locked jaw backdrop,
the bright lights, the wooden skull.
Unless Shakespeare dies, he'll
be here with an impression of you.

A cinder lights
the rough incense, thin, papery
and smoke twilled.
The sandalwood is all
you have in the ink-black—
you keep insisting
you have beautiful dreams
as they smoke,

when they are quite terrible.
You awake and wish
you had never lived,
unless I can recall you
quite young in your oyster, before
your defence mechanism
crystallized calcium, layer upon layer,
prophesied like nacre,
formed a pearl.

Acknowledgement (Ossia)

I don't cry here
anymore,
the tears have turned
to salt on an old woman's
parchment face,
she became a pillar
of beeswax,
she has an unclaimed wit,
her wick has never been burned,
her lilies in the garden grow wild.

Nobody said,
"I do," and ate the potatoes with gravy,
no one stretched out their hand
with a band
of limitless gold.
(Binding the unexpected.)

She is an archangel now,
fluttering about the house—
her white hair flecked
and distressed
as a vintage memoir.

Humanitarian Objections

The Shoe Tree

They say the heroin addicts
in this town
tied all these shoes together
by hand,
and threw them into the
branches of a tree.

There must have been
a hundred pairs
in a large elm
full of shoes,
each one speaking of someone
without shoes.

Your name was Friday.
You were sitting in the
doorway when I found you,
you had walked a long way,
and your shoes were
dusty and torn,
the tongues gaping wide
over your bare feet.

There was a thought
that someone should buy
you another pair,
and should that
someone be me?

You were a lost boy,
and I was a shoe tree,
waving my arms,
insisting there are lots of shoes
for everyone.

Dragons in the Swamp

I thought skunk cabbage
was as white inside
as a sepulchre,
with a stench of the dead,
and rigid, upright
with nowhere to lay its lead.

The dragon of the swampy
black mud depths
is not depravity kind—
yet shall sin unwind
in her arsenic boots.
She had a cadmium modem,
so she told me,
that made her connected
to every other living thing.

They all dashed and bashed
her head,
until it was bent
and yellow—still breathing,
but putrescent,
still living, but unwilling,
unyielding.

Dragons in the Caves

There was a long tunnel
of connected caves,
where dragons lived by the sea.
Their mica ores flamed like nostrils.

I found the morning
where the smoke was rising
from their sulphurous mouths;
I found the evening,
the colour of copper moths,
and sinewy green flesh—

What unknown light is walking
down the road?
It must be only a stranger's light;
if it had relative form or
were in any way known to them,
they would swallow
the poor person whole,
unless he was hiding
in a hole somewhere.

Before the Fire

There was a vandalised wall
between my heart
and my mind.
The graffiti coloured wall drove
believers underground
for fear of persecution.

Few continued on in this vein
of silence over spiritual matters,
of quiet church,
humming the great hymns of the faith
in reservation
behind bolted doors.

When the wall came down,
missionaries came
like tiny people,
only for us to tell them
there was no watermelon
on this side of the wall before now.

They talked about Creation,
but we had only heard
of evolution.
Their script
was to smile, accept us,
and invite us in.

We were an acceptable darkness,
with poverty of religion,
no candle to see by,
like being married
with no wedding rings
and no church.

Then there was a bonfire,
and people surrounded it
with their hands stretched out;
better to be warm, we thought,
than cold.
Now we could sing louder.

Alleluiah, alleluiah
rang over the hills
of Germany:
it was a sad and glorious song.

The Cupboard

The doors of my cupboard
are an insect's wings,
small, illusive,
and things of flight—
catching light and darkness, swinging
open so everyone can see
what I keep hidden—
the neat Ikea bowls and plates
in orange and blue.

I thought they were relatively ordinary,
as a dragonfly over a lake,
nothing to mention,
but others, with nostalgia, finger them,
running their fingers over porcelain,
and put the bowls on their heads
like Jewish prayer caps—
then parade around,
boasting of plates in bright colours.

Frosted with emotion,
there is nothing in my mind.
It has all been emptied
and pilfered bare by scavengers
who saw a hole in the cupboard door
and helped themselves.

They even tried to put
their own things in my cupboard,
while I practiced meditation
as a skilful cover-up.

Now they fly like insects
on insect's wings—
tiny, whining, and growing smaller
in the distance.

If I Was Frost

Dedicated to Anna Frost

I knew it was almost winter
when the ground I walked on
was starched and stunted with ambiguity.

There was a mist over the trees,
like an iron's steam,
or a halo's sheen,
or a vision of a train appearing
and blurring the scene.

If I was my great-great-grandmother
she would not be less reticent,
less dulcet, or less articulate
than I in green—
the colour of an undersea garden.

She sits at the kitchen table
and can crochet—
there is always much to do,
but she finds the time.
No one ever compliments
her work, but no one paid her either.

If I was Anna Frost,
my heart would linger
behind me in the field of snow,
because she is too shy to see
the future.

My mind would move
from room to room,
because it is like dancing.

My arms would rise up
to explain a mutual story
about one of our own.

My legs would fly out
in sinewy regality
like I was a flapper dancing the
Charleston,
when really I had died.

I would lay flat,
and covered with frost
as a winter's landscape,
frozen hair,
dressed in my wedding gown,
missional ivory.

The Fading Town

You'll get used to me,
mile upon mile,
you'll get used to my crown,
glittering beneath the ground.

I died a long time ago,
an elderly persecuted ego,
with a city built up within me,
and a fading town on the outside.

The trampled outskirts
were far into the marshlands,
and the herons waved their weeping wings,
and swallows croaked—
the frogs would sing.
The victuals of seed
and steel-red berry, beyond
the unutterable wounding
of latent hunger.

You'll get used to the mighty Stave,
thundering into the open hands
of the powerless,
of the long winding roads
in the damp country,
and the agricultural bushel.

The horses sniff the wind—
they are travellers too,
galloping into the lower field
at night, like we are powerful,
of intellectual orbits
like the long line
of poplars striking the sky.

Weep Salt

I am a foreigner in my own country—
my starch gives me
a pleasant consistency,
and I am stirred again and again
over the portable stove.

There are oats in my bones,
my character insists.
Some women weep salt
while they cook;
they could scarcely
hope for dark bread
and now make fibrous porridge.

The liquefied starch
is sweet as water,
and our minds
were hoping they would be
unaffected by its absence.

I am a foreigner in my own country—
without my rough bowl of gruel.

Ballads

Last Words From A Weaver's Basket

It's just you and me,
when the moon lies low
and the odd little winds blow,
here at our wood cabin by the sea.

It's our moment together,
when the foghorn sound fades
through deep wooded shores forever,
and the ancient ghost ships wager.

Ships would find their way
by the island's undertow.
They would 'round the bay
to the old red lighthouse's lantern glow.

The fog winds blew,
when the sky rained dew
over the tips of the woodland fir,
the weaver's basket drips with woven myrrh.

Spirit weavers stand,
as harmonic as the land—
in and out like the tide—
do the shell-brittle hands bide.

It's just you and me,
still-weaving the sea,
from the heather on the hill
to the salt-hued gulls' bill.

The rocks were rough and coarse
beneath the spirit weavers' hands,
and they were graphite bands
departing in cedar-carved force.

There was a garden for a mile
just for you and me;
sit with me for awhile,
while the lilies weave by the sea.

By the mossy shore, the ocean sighs,
where a covert cove hides,
its fingers upon the harpsichord;
resplendent is the light through the plank boards.

Wait with me for a tear
while I echo here—
spirits weaving a basket into a braid,
sit here, while I am afraid.

When there is no more sun, and no more eves,
and the earth bows down,
we will be sinking into the ground.
Sit here, while the spirit weaves.

I let you hold my hand
between sea and land,
where the pulse beats fine;
there is enough dulse for you and I.

It's just our last mussel pearl
for the sinking world,
while the wild wind blows,
and the glittering river flows.

I will not love lend,
but my fingers break and bend
with the spirit weavers, and boldly fare—
leaving behind my cold broken rocking chair.

The round wood door into paradise
lies low to the earth, but in a fever
who would unearth the gold weaver
and her basket: who would ever find it?

There is a gracious door for you and I
that we found by and by;
don't forget to listen to the brine,
and decipher her salty rhyme.

See the women on the shore there
that have turned into stones;
there is someone singing into the foam—
and the spirit weavers are braiding her hair.

Ballad of the Oboe Player

"Darling," said my mother,
winsome in the sun and rain,
"You'll need clothing of salvation,
and the seams will make me pray.

"There's nothing in my mind
that would constitute a cure for sin,
to make you autumn clothing,
to not let the winter in.

"There's nothing in my soul's lament
that could purchase hope for you,
just a moulding potato, bent,
and a lettuce in the dew."

That was in Indian Summer,
then came almost winter's snow,
"Daughter, there's a legend runner
of the life before the fall crows."

Tiny little elbows, and tiny little knees,
besides the mattress bare
is rent with filth and fleas,
you're sleeping in my care.

If I had no clothes to make you
it would embarrass Mother Earth,
she would not let you run naked too,
she'd make you clothes of buckskin mirth.

When the snows had fallen glittering,
and winter had begun, fiercely beside
the icicles, were chickadees twittering,
over the clothing I had never worn outside.

In the house, I could wear velvet,
at the table, I wear pearls,
but what good is finery to catch a rabbit
and skin it for the soup of earls.

I couldn't go to school and write,
the stack of books was piled high,
like cakes I couldn't have at noon's light
or mandarins whose skins I dared not pry.

I couldn't go to church,
my shoes had holes too,
in front of all the other little boys and girls;
my vitamins leaked through.

Finally my mother stated, "Brawny,
I will measure you,"
and she measured every scrawny
limb, my waist and ankles too.

A tick-tock-ticking sounded
the wood grandfather clock,
busy were we, without being hounded,
yes, now we were busy with our material stock.

Busy enough not to let the wind know,
for a secret announced to the wind
is a tall tale to all upon its flaming show,
instead of the coal light of a cinder.

So here I stand, a statue girl,
in potato sacks I would relay,
whose mother could not string a pearl,
but played me music all the day.

The winter was the worst that year,
it snowed 'till March, I would wager,
the men would sit and drink a beer,
the women take a food voucher.

The snow lay in drifts to the top of the roof thatch,
and we melted the snow to drink water;
we cooked the last of the rice and lit beeswax,
then made soap from the olive oil to give lather.

In spring, the water with a heron's feet pooled,
and eddied in the basin,
whether your day's work was good or cruel,
there were sausages in casings.

A wolf or two howled outside the shellac
of our small wood home,
but there was nothing that we lacked
except salvation's bodice and a shell comb.

"So get out the iron," she said, "the wool,
and the cotton. Make yourself a modest girl,
who has two pigtails, bobbins, and can wear pearls.
Sew yourself a skirt by the candle's wax pool."

I saw my father sitting on the patriarchal chair,
there was newspaper for a hearth fire
that he had left in piles there;
my mother, not a moment wasted, not a tyre.

She had a porcelain doll with a little head,
and it wore green skirts, with a carol book;
she loved it and would not sell it for thread.
It was the most expensive thing we had for looks.

My father bought a clarinet at the music store,
it was made for a prince, but he gave it to me as a gift;
it made a strange sound that carried over the floor,
and my mother sat dead, and listened to my thrift.

If her fingers were saving grace, they bought my reeds;
she made attractive bead bangles,
a scarf or a hat, or sewed cilantro seeds
in a garden of flowering guardian angels.

I could play the clarinet within the band,
neat and sensible clothing went with the olive soap,
so I memorized notes on the music stand,
and then the band master gave me an oboe.

My mother pulled the hair from the horse's tail
to stuff my mattress, made my quilt;
now we had something beyond the grail
of butter and bread, and softened guilt.

The reed resounded in the silence lonely
of the shadows, and the smiles;
we thought lovely music was like being paid in honey,
then he bought her a loom, though she was in denial.

The mourning sound had an innocuous thrill
as the loom began to fly, as the lake became the melted water,
as the oboe would play, in lilting trill,
as only a prince would wear his alma matter.

As a girl wore her salvation, sewn by her mother,
a lavender sachet in her drawer and wool stockings,
a prince was clothed in the music of the oboe,
and resplendent was its tawny mocking.

There was a lyrical pursuit that would lead,
so it seemed to a musical pauper,
but was really a poor girl with a heady reed
in one meagre song after another.

One day, I would humbly place
my instrument on my knees on the stage,
and the orchestra would pause,
as I melted souls with Gabriel's Oboe.

Earth Talks to her Creator

The Evolution of Covid

I.   Loved One

My day stretches
like a cat under a Freeman maple,
an invisible canopy over my heart,
covering love and hate,
Wagner in so many ways.

I was once a cloistered stair,
then nipped in the cream bud.
A blind woman there,
I traveled in coals,
the dark was my cloak,
my bodice was stars,
my hair was fair as smoke,
as a spring moon before Mars,
my eyes were rims of clear gold.

But now I bloom—
the sea rages, roses dip in the salt,
the cold red flowers succumb
by night . . .
Their reticent fingers
reach for covert grandeur.

II. Lover

The dark mire,
it has spies, it has stones
with seven eyes,
and rock gardens' bones.

With fountains of wordless dew,
the moments blithe blossom,
the cultivated lesson,
the silent shrew.

Every flower of the valley
blooms under the mountain's shadow,
the rosa and the lillian
are but names for flowers.

I meet the Black Maples in the dark,
a cultivated heir,
but the day winds through dry grass,
and the fields of purple clover.

III. Loved One

I slept beside a wall—
two feet thick,
there was romance
in the heart of Canada.

When I spent the tall night
in Quebec,
bravely clinging to my new
ideals amid the old.

The facades in the towns
were of ancient brick and stone,
the statues wept glory—
the cobblestones echoed.

In an art shop,
they gifted me with
a few prints of old castles
with Striped Maples reflecting in pools
and men on horseback.

IV. Lover

We ate at a table that was
set for two,
with brioches and cheese—
they let us eat outdoors.

Only for a moment or two,
then Vodka was brought
in a lemon water bowl
to wash our hands.

They say it kills disease,
that is why some drink,
they kill the nasty vermin
while drinking wine.

At the finest bed and breakfast
there is the white chamber; all in white,
our chamber where we stay in peaceful
dreams of former times, fading antiques.

V.   Loved One

The White Chamber
only echoes the covert love
and fear of touch, the distance—
the need for breathing space.

Then there is the Sea Chamber
of sea and salt,
of the sun-bleached tide,
and driftwood pale.

Lilies grow en masse off the porch
of this old house by the ocean,
wild lilies, lilies of the valley,
lilies of the sea, the shells leave
their remains.

The depths of art have
flung you with great briny force,
now you face your sole salty
witness, the oracle of
the vine and mountain.

VI. Lover

I found you under a Red Maple
effortlessly gliding in a pond.
You are adorned with opal teardrops
they sparkle in your eyes and swan down.

They garner your feathered neck
when the seasons change
to depict birth and death—
you change also, spinning arranged

away on a leaf as a dove.
Dropping hints
of first love,
I calm to diminuendos.

My beloved,
eyes bright
and your heart
a bed of dimming coals.

VII. Loved One

There are grapes in the vineyard,
and I am sweet;
a dulcet movement
by composers unheard.

When the afternoon
spills its lake perfume,
the water runs down
my skin to the ground.

I am oiled with olive's toil,
I am impermeable;
I resist all moisture,
while diluting the finest of oils.

Rose hip, bergamot, and cassia
are mine;
cypress, cedar, and eucalyptus
are yours.

VIII.   Lover

I live in a house of trees,
they cool me with shade,
they rivet me in sunlight,
they drip on me in rain.

You live in a house of many walls,
with a cindery hearth,
and red bricks
that have turned black from fires.

There are tall dark windows
hiding unrecovered things;
things that the world is hiding,
things that the world has mourned.

In this house, there has been
many a teapot filled with tea,
many a pauper poor,
many a page has held his ear to the door,
many a king can see.

IX. Loved One

That was my arugula
growing placidly
in decent green dress
with a crocheted collar.

The garden tapestry expanded
with the rainfall of late summer;
the clouds amassed
and passed in pillars of stone grey.

There were the seedlings
leveraging their height on stakes,
there were the potatoes,
hidden beneath the dark black earth,
they were speaking above ground,
reaching for light, witnessing.

Clamouring toward the sky
were the string beans,
skinny and nasally whining
in both yellow and wax.

There was a silent moment
when I contemplated
that all vegetables and their nutrients
have wont to grow,
to be mature,
to stretch the soul.

X.   Lover

I am deciduous, I am upright
and massive—
I tolerate the emptiness of
a water-less existence, and drought.

Renowned for my display every year
in green, orange, red, and yellow
all the leaves are resplendent
against the blue.

I regain my strength in spring, and
change my colours in autumn,
then wither and die,
my browned sepia leaves falling to
paper the frosted ground.
I will never forget you,
though I am burned and ploughed
beneath the earth.

I hearken to darkness and snow,
I become death like a dance
that I may be baptized
beneath your eternity.

XI.   Loved One

The Vine Maple was gnarled, and
thought I would climb its myriad branches
and wait for Christ's return,
languid with my hair hanging down.

My hair fell down into a spring-fed pool,
from the pool hopped a green frog,
on the rock scuttled a Patrika lizard,
in the mountains roamed a bearded Billy goat.

I could wait like Old Israel
with oil in my lamp, dressed in flax linen,
and a horn to my lips,
to sound the last moment in alarm.

But I preferred to strum and sing,
venerating time on the copper harp,
playing interference
to disaster, advocating.

XII. Lover

The Silver Maple
has undersides like a fin,
flashing highlights in sable
despite various hues of green.

Against the dark,
there is light here,
pinpointing its various
luxury names.

Mountain Maple grows
into a subtle fall with
natural flair for existence
harvest hues in orange, in mist.

The wagon wheel in broken wood
with iron rims
has been here since the house was built,
and the wheel dating back to the 1800's.

XIII.   Loved one

I see a man,
he is clothed in white,
beautiful in the dark,
walking stark against the panorama of night.

The stars are blinding and abundant
as he walks quietly under the tree,
the Japanese Maple rustles
its dark crimson leaves.

No one can see him but me;
he is the Maple Tree Angel—
when I called his name,
the tree moved with a new wind.

It was a light wind, almost invisible
and very small—
diminutive with meekness;
it is the wind that stirs the leaves.

XIV.   Lover

The Paperbark Maple
peels dramatically
in cinnamon coloured bark,
scarlet in the fall landscape.

She was a make-shift missionary
to the Chinese
and left her mark like a bite
on a sharp-nosed pit viper.

It fermented in the wetlands
among the bog sedges, cattails, and water lilies.
The mandarin trees were as old
as the earth itself, and wore orange-coloured robes.

The piece "Nola" was from the Earth's grandmother
and could no longer be played
on a narrow upright piano,
with peeling wood,
with keys missing
and out-of-tune notes.

There is no hope
if nothing changes,
there is an old withered aloe,
and a dying song.

I hoped we could tame
your prodigal ugliness,
but never thought the ugly
duckling would turn to swan.

XV. Loved One

Almost tempted to play,
I saw my error,
as a true musician would;
even when the tree is young . . .

I would play only the golden Samick.
I would string a minute ebony sonata,
I am sun-beaten with Mozart,
and composers find love in my branches.

The birds score their notes,
a treble cleft is scribbled down,
and bass—the effulgence of earth
in the Ash-leaf Maple's compound leaves.

The music waited,
it had time, I had power.
There was not room for my piano,
with standing room only in the hall.

XVI.   Lover

If you have given,
if you have loved quietly in silence,
your pen minimalist at best
scratches the surface of the page,
the shades are lowered,
the room is dark.
The waiting is long;
the days of summer come,
the heat stills,
and sweats from the sidewalk.

There are people passing by,
they walk to and fro wearing colourful
masks, and their words are cut off
in a survivalist world of fear.

The beat of the drum lures them
into minion obedience,
while the dames dare
revolution songs.

Softly the song rises
in the middle of the night:
"Kill the beast, spill his blood,
slit his throat."

XVII.   Loved One

Here I stand,
statuesque,
with sixty warriors
at my side—

They are virtuous to defend me,
they have passed the law of love,
what goes before,
and what follows.

Can we hold our morality
in our hands,
when it trickles through our fingers
like salt water—it is bitter.

Our lips purse at our former thoughts
of caste and rank,
of social class and the deprived—
now all eyes stare hollowly.

We worship the trees,
we adore the Douglas Maple's shade,
and you for awhile supporting a wide-spreading crown:
a Big Leaf Maple with curtain calls.

Auditions are held of people
to walk in your park;
ruffled leaves turn various
shades of green as the wind blows.

XVIII.   Lover

Stop, O wind–
you Pharisee breathing your
redemption of after-life.
Death tempts me but I believe

it is the sleep.
Sleep soundly, sleep softly—
dream lucidly
in the deep.

The music stills,
I am mute now;
it is the winter of my life,
and it has come for me, swiftly.

Sleep!—

Four hours ago you were
a dove in a tree,
three hours ago you lay dead,
a white rose at your breast.

There was a music in your soul
the very poignant dream
of the very young, you see,
when it sounds,
it will bypass all the reasons
you want to die,
and let you live on.

XIX.   Loved One

You have liberty then—
you have died and risen—
you climbed the secret stair
before morning into the gold-green lair.

The passage of mournful eyes
and fluttering leaves
beckoned you—from an ivory tower
to the light of the moon.

There would be no death here—
no mortal corpse—
no pale velvet coffin—
no undertaker to dig our graves.

Our thoughts shall live,
our madness stings,
our voices sing,
though nameless now we be.

Our thoughts shall live again,
in faery, fancy, fable;
the gilded lily shall ring
like a sanguine gong.

When the Sky is Falling

Skyfall Sonnet

Do not in stagnant water flow, but swim
in the river with clear springs—at the brim
of sunlight's last clean sweep of sky, as lone
as the moons of Saturn, hung one by one
in your Creator hands, turn brevity
to song and valour emanates from this:
that the mind is theologically
inclined to do war and battles forthwith.
Take out one's sword, and triumph!—slay the foe
at this last hour, when earth is falling low;
into a field, death's horse now circles round
and ends the rider's life on gravestone mound.
What richness would this world to all direct,
that in its bosom, neither could protect.

The Altar

You are the altar
on which I am sacrificed on rough stones,
praying like a bird in a cage,
steeling my forehead as a farmer does
when his plough must go forward,
seeing the sun drop in the sky.

And the clouds ever-move,
sculpted by the master.
Drifting from one thought
to the next, composed.

The rain falls, on dormant
worlds and high-strung gardens.
A cellist sits on the wall
and plays toward evening.

You are the womb of life
and when I am born I am firmly in your grasp.
Holding me to the breast
is the mother of life,
and the breath in me must go forward…
'till death lays me in a field.

Reflective Dreams

The Mirror of a Droplet

There is a wooden boat
floating on the pond
of water lilies.
I drift
through the waters of time,
I am lucid, and my spirit
revels too
in this glory.

There is the fog over the deep,
the chirp and creep,
the nest and burrow,
the farmer's furrow,
the bead and drop,
the song and call.

There is rest and work,
walking on and on…
over plank board pathways,
over cedar chip walks,
over bridges,
and over the water floating by.

The Mirror of a Soul

There is a rain,
drops on the pond
of soul lilies.
I am a solo goose call
through the waters sublime,
I am reticent, and my spirit
drips like drops of mist.

There is the silence;
the chirp and creep are stilled,
the nest and burrow are filled,
the farmer's furrow runs deep,
the bead and drop are sweet,
the song and call of feet.

There is much to dream,
plodding on and on…
over people's regrets
dipping like ducks in a line,
over winsome failures
and bridges of the mind,
and over the water lilies floating by.

Requiems in the Mist

Requiem for a Gothic Spire (Notre Dame)

Lying beside the navy River Seine
was the gate of the Lady of Heaven;
her warm Madonna smile was bread leaven
to all who loved her son's essential vein.
There was no forged crucible with blood stained
hands, without being pierced by his brethren,
for he was one of us; we were forgiv'n
by his very heart despised, sapphire reign.
There—a ring of unending gold as fire,
a melodious sound came from the wood
of relinquished cross, now crucified stone
played on the third morn as a fragrant lyre
of old, the pages were turned as we would
in the valley of a prophet's dead bones.

What word would speak and raise the spire to sky;
what hope would glisten as the morning dew?
There was a church that blazed its colours true,
linen crevices were indigo dyed
and hailing from Europe, the prayer would rise
that from a deity drew kingdoms new,
to rest upon the heads of saints glass-blue,
quiet patience and perseverance tried.
I would repeal the curse that rests bereft
beneath my hand, for I the ink and quill
that wrote each word of the scriptures was one
that stood in souls of time with my request.
I would not break or violate your will
lest you asking lack something, come undone.

The organ thundered out, we lift our chant
within Our Lady's alabaster stone,
with rushing river by the island's moan;
the true living remnant would not recant.
Brilliant prairie grasses of Miscanthus,
Pennisetum, Stipa, with flowers grown
as Echinacea and Achilleas' throne.
The iron of this sanctuary rusts
its bounty in the hearts of those who sing,
their low carol carried o'er the threshold
where other flowers tarry due nearby
and their waxen perfume unyielded stings.
But the brocaded ceilings were of gold,
and song's sound mingled with the tears and cries.

A flame towered in the dark, its blood spurts
with a vice of midnight, now dying blade
that from a steel sword swiftly did away
with all mild dissidence and fear of hurt.
We were no more, we leaned and grandly cursed
the ground we had once walked upon, in sways
of lowly field, and revelled lovely-made
from vestments of the air that saline pursed
the tide upon the beach of Paris's front.
She was wont to be wearing red, silence
brought tidings of her reputation forth;
she was a queen of the night, took the brunt
of their insults to death. Knights took violence
from strangers of other realms to gain worth.

There was a hint of burning cinder there,
beyond cathedral's levelled paradigm;
there was the sound of sun and moon resigned
where pigeons roost in alcoves of star air.
What were their last words as these silver stairs
filled with smoke from some guilty humankind;
a glass of lemon water with the rind
sat on the old wood table with no care.
There was no fault, no blame in stone was set,
no blinding flame has seared our coral minds—
their deep porous thoughts, staid with minerals.
But now our hearts, reduced to ash, are met
with dark realities of other kinds,
the Gothic spire was once ethereal.

Not one pale stone was left upon the next,
and so no crucified corpse remained there,
there was no evidence in dragon's lair,
only an ashen kind remembers text
from a burned down Bible's vast lexicon.
If I was to pour pure oil in my hair,
the fruit of virgin olive break and tear;
the black circle from its branch, comely vexed,
would be on coming out with pearl drop glass.
The poorest girl would now hit the high notes
and circle as a falcon, bird of prey,
for you thought to make them victims of class,
you hoped they would try calling you, emote,
and fiery burned them to the ground that day.

To raise the dead from every ladened curse,
the gargoyles, covered with soot from the fire,
return to the oak of youth's golden spire,
remember the covenant you made first:
to love no other but me, lest you thirst
and drink of another cistern, you tire—
the level of purity I require,
too difficult for anyone but Christ.
So he will be your prize, your figurehead,
he will be set on high, and in the rocks
of hellish night, where burns your soulish branch.
There entered not one tree to this blood-red
rose, just a child came by with blond dreadlocks,
swung under a Maritime Pine, then blanched.

Requiem for a Solitary Unicorn

The song of a dying white unicorn—
he bowed his horn in meadow flowers spun,
and flee not the coming wrath, neither run.
From his brow unfurled the steeple, his horn.
There was a text of prophecy then borne
to earth within his vestal silver frame,
the word spoken from ancients was his name
and in a rustic stable, the child born.
Rhema would guard his cherished golden head
and beams of light fell from his mercy eyes
to oft transcend the poverty of earth,
to feed the multitudes on coarse dark bread
and read the signs of the celestial skies.
To apprehend the curse, there is no curse.

What novice could hide herself in a cell
and know the living presence as a flame,
to walk by candlelight medieval lane;
to hearing ears, mystics' chants and prayers fell.
Read the song again, this book is poem:
there is a repetition of its thread,
there is salvation in its bodice bred,
there is the hope of an eternal home.
Who built these stone walls of fierce workmanship?
Was there a foreman, mason on the site;
the very brick denotes his pay. Who paid?
Some man of bright wisdom or fine wealth, it
pleased him, such a great castle, where no blight
would devastate your cares and hopes, or raid.

No one can batter these walls, brokenness
is not the form of a healthy woman:
lexicon from the glance of sainthood wan,
the nuns protect her vows in eagerness
to win her favour. St. Clare is patron
of this fragile heart prepared for vastness
of a heather tundra, windy, restless;
there are dreams within the green eyes of sun
through the windows of the cathedral tall—
the light that falls on us in silken streams,
anointing of the green olive oil tree
in a lonely chapel, wooden and small,
that overcame death and decay for beams
of fluent light and laughter. Sit with me.

I sit on the bench. I am in the hall.
I travel in ions of turquoise hues;
I mesmerize my audience with blues,
melancholia sells tickets to all.
There is a long line of wealthy patrons
who want to buy their way into this world
of theatrical curtain calls and twirls
of lines, rehearsals, pinafore aprons.
We have our way of crossing the dark stage,
there's a rope holding the curtain, which sways
in midnight colour of deep navy blue.
Who stands in the shadows? Is she nymph, sage,
in darkness. Lighting the candle in ways
that are now spirit-led and keep us true.

Her head is high, she thinks and rises next,
speaking her lines to us like a sharp horn
that catapulted her into black thorns,
with a bright trumpet call to rouse the dead.
If the thistle of criticism had
not frightened her she would have been quite calm,
the tide of sea would sweep in as a balm—
salt, but her voice rose to a fevered mad
and obscene tone; it was a fearful deck
she had been dealt. The blackened Queen of Spades
gathered her powers, and regal, she spoke:
I am the land, the earth writhes, its slim neck,
reputation that would save from Hades.
Mock me not, for earth disappears as smoke.

We sought her favour like a drum that beats
its rueful pilgrimage to the stone heights
of mountains, with rocky canyons, and brights
of sunset upon dusk, the bard her teats,
and weaver spun this glory as a song.
Where the beat kept on, we gladly in line
followed the mother's milky breast, a sign
of her truth, gold lion's mane, and tail long.
When no real lion roars, then no one tastes
the soup and bread of her table, no one
believes she is just. Maybe they refuse
to eat what she prepared, in lower castes
of denial and want (they say I'm done);
in homely ways the haggard beggars choose.

The well-fed are not eager, bones and skin,
for the court of the prophets, where Rhema
bows the unicorn's horn, dazzling schema
of the inner world. For you go within
to find peace from despair, and bow your head
in rest upon a Saviour's breast. Molech's
night of the star's soul gives you no solace,
though you toss and turn upon your plaid bed.
The horn was righteous blessing on your day,
but you preferred the night of pallid fright,
who would prefer a nightmare to a dream?
The ship of your mind sailed into the bay—
a way to find unicorn's linen-white
side or have her sew the lovely shell seam.

Requiem for an Aging Sea

I swept the tidal mass unto the shore
since beginnings of the earth: land and sea;
since sun and moon began, and first-born tree
was rooted in the soil of rich brown lore.
There was no stolid unforgiveness here,
there's no hand of navy retribution
where we must force bloody revolution
of scarlet martyred front, the woman's tier.
The ocean was your first love, when men left
for the sea: sailors with no worldly cares
except vast liquid horizon, dulcet
moon dipping the waters, and sunlight deft
brimming o'er the wooden orange barrel;
and the mast with its tall stalwart concept.

If the sea would cry out in white anguish,
the waves would crash in tide upon the rock,
cragging paths of the shore without prism smocked
solace, the water would be a British
maid, upon beauteous isle oft the coast,
lapping the sand of minute grey and brown,
standing there in her apron, her mouth frowned;
she looked out to sea, awaiting the lost
ship, willing it to return from the storm.
It would be a mother wound, the poison
of a war that was their debt, and the loss
of so many lives. She was fragile form—
waiting there and never moved, her crimson
mouth still singing his song, stone-cold with moss.

The lithe seabirds fly and she stands there still,
her hands with long fingers to play the harp,
the fishermen with nets would harvest carp,
while she would strum trees oft the cliffs with ill
winds that would whip and blow the rocky shore,
the women's skirts would dance in coloured dress
refining tastes of men put to the test—
to love women like the sea, banish whores
from London streets, and taking daughters by
the hand to revel in the marriage
of sea and land. These are of old, ancient
as sailor's navigation had star-ties.
The bride and groom got into their carriage,
circling planets, ivory innocent.

The dark waves and depths were darker than land,
the moon was elegantly fair of face,
the stars stretched out their whitened Kenmare lace,
the green of Ireland waved its gloved hand.
The daffodil of Wales bowed iron head,
and England stood, a cathedral of stone,
with panes of stained glass through which the light shone
with anointing, this wine-like honeyed mead—
and touch of grace with healing in its wings.
The Great Black-backed Gulls flew up, and soared high
above the brine, the cool dank filmy air—
they lived scavenging, but their wise call rings
with a life of salt unmarked by the dye
of indigo-scarred sea, old and austere.

What was this tree of time that grew on land—
each bark-wrought branch a son with brave courage—
to seek the light, and try to lessen scourge,
integrity to their last breath; and hands
that fashioned carpentry with saws and nail.
The art of wood was resurrected mast,
and homes of quality were handsome cast,
with furniture whose legend does not fail.
Their wives were cared for when they stayed on land,
but men had dreams that made their sea-eyes wild,
they dreamt of naval ports, of setting sail—
the Riviera beckoned the Captain:
foreign harbours, oriental silk mild,
sailing the coast when the wind would not fail.

Africa called to men in their sleep, dreams
made them listless and seeking adventure,
they left for their oceanic nurture,
of the power that moves men from the cream
of life, a wooden house with garden flow'rs—
for the life of violence and war's red fruit,
for the hard clasp of the guns, swords, and brutes.
Their ships would sail from emerald towers:
the waves oft the shore, the depths, the silver
fish, the harvest of the sea—liniment,
a sun-streaked weary sky would set each night,
oils of eucalyptus and lavender
were balm of kindness, green eyes, imminent
to regain their blue-streaked morning-tide light.

The sea has aged with the drawing of time;
it grows restless now and creation broods
far under the water, whales die in moods,
and struggle to reach the surface of crimes
against them and their habitat. Their breath
cries out into the open—we cry save
the whales, while English boats upon the wave
of the modern world laugh. The kelp tide's death
crackles with green iridescence and salt,
once-food does not nourish us anymore,
we hunger for the minerals of sea—
but she is lost, dark-winged like the night's cult
as our dry bones hit the ocean's sand floor—
we scorn their value to humanity.

Requiem for a Royal Rose

Perhaps the speaker should be introduced:
departed from Greece, the far distant land,
where knighthood made him vow to win the hand
extended in favour, sea eyes, lucid—
of his lady. They would know him only
as her one handsome Duke of Edinburgh.
His calling might have been regal might, curbed,
to taste the flowers that emit honey,
to rest bouquet on whitened baby's breath,
and to be father of both the lily
and the rose. For there are swords unwieldy,
and yet the love streams down, bright and bereft,
of our days upon the earth, and how we
walked through desert sands and through snowy fields.

He chose to speak, and this is what he spoke:
chance forbade this favour to have his voice,
duty forbade the end to have a choice,
his children's Bible names are what he wrote.
He was not scribe, nor poet, nor a vice,
he was a consort, yet rule was quiet
leader, not daunting or pre-imminent,
but lilting his hoarse laugh rang more than twice
at the birth of a son, through these hallowed
now deserted halls. Each child would grow, leave,
for their own adult nefarious reels.
There was a book of Scripture, that mellowed
into dusty old regimented leaves,
turned grey doctrine into the grace that heals.

For a petal to fall from a rose bud
it must first blossom in royal red hue;
they crowned you first and always in the blue
garden valley—where the prophecy's nudge
would enliven and wake us from death first;
recall the mountains—of sapphire martyred.
You were a Queen of domains uncharted,
and minions hid themselves beneath your skirts.
There was a ringing of the depth of rest—
in all your nation's wisdom, and your smile
never betrayed your deepest warmest heart.
There was rose of cordiality's crest
in every traversed field and forest mile,
you, in each hospitable gesture, art.

Her dark head bent over each sonorous
word, each syllable lent itself to sound,
the height of golden understanding crowned
beneath a tenet king incredulous—
His will to teach would be expedient:
just then, meek understanding of a verse
so solemn, vigorous, so full of mirth—
made his façade no longer lenient.
There was a poem, sacred, resting there,
beneath her ivory breast, a nation
signed their signature into her white throat,
the reputation of a crown, best here
where the brown falcons rise at her station,
and "All Hail!" becomes majority vote.

The rose grew up the Windsor Castle wall
breathing wine, it will stand at attention
in red salute, military mention
with glossy mahogany in the hall.
Her figure was reflected in the glass:
there were no entwined figures in a tree;
spirit of love hath at long last slain me—
I will not die—I hope but not to fast
beneath the ground, when all is lost about.
Shall I be departed, or shall veiled you?
Deep-dark rugs shall no more hear or pardon
resting footsteps, my voice shall not ring out.
English bluebells fashioned themselves in twos
for your tiara, and in your gardens.

She bowed her head and proclaimed eight days rest.
For all of England was the duty mourned:
she married every royal child in gown;
the call was that she nursed them at her breast.
He forbade that one stray drop fall from this
precious vial of a Queen in gossamer.
Ruby diadem and service silver
appeared at her edict, knighted thistles
in several orders bent frosted heads.
Lord and lady, sword and shield now immersed
in her regal kingdom, ornate and bold,
took from their packs needle and navy threads,
for the sea eyes would command their commerce,
while endorsing plum fairy tales untold.

In the dark wood where the blithe fairies hide
a noiseless purple feather fell to earth;
from under the ribcage of linear birth
that blessed diminutive blossomed bride.
The bird it came from no one knew of lived—
for it was not a bird of song, but one
of prey, and on the hunt led the way on
through the dank woodlands of trees in olive.
The horses thundered down, they braved the toil
of war and on from English soil they broached
enemies undeterred—to leave, reckoned,
blood red. Fleur-de-lis ampulla their oil—
they were a solemn front in royal coach,
silvered by death, opaque blossoms beckoned.

Requiem for the Queen's Swan

The wall beside the Queen's pond was adept
at keeping undesirables out; swans
flew in and landed with their huge wing spans:
enough to break a man's arm if unkempt.
The eldest woman on castle grounds sat
and watched them every day for silken hours,
her hair was white as snow, her eyes water
blue, as she sat and stroked a long-haired cat.
Her wildest prayers she would enunciate,
and her hands were painfully gnarled I guessed,
she believed transformation was reeling
its answers in the form of art quite late—
the swans were poets: spirits effortless
at self-love, where she had little feeling.

She wrote like the web and was very old,
of a spider's haunt, the delicate dew
hung from each strand of her mind, not askew,
although her bun contained the wisps of cold.
Elegant swans hated the velvet hounds,
the populace thought they were causing war,
disastrous occurrences, even far
off prophecies had already been found
innocent by church theology, they
only predict the future, not cause it.
Merciless, blood hounds chased and arrested
miserable chaste birds and made them prey;
people of Poland were not opposed, writ
words given up, eating succulent flesh.

For swans are faithful creatures, dedicate
their lives to one spouse, and raise their cygnets
splashing into the waters, calm there met:
their words are harsh and hiss, relegated
to a library stack with fearsome beaks.
Habitual mornings are somewhat poor;
half past seven, they arrive asking for
breakfast. Their host in a house is the meek
Parish Priest, he put the swans under his
protection from the twelfth century's blood:
it is illegal to harm a swan, white,
black, or any consort—webbed feet, a Liszt
in sleight of hand upon the keys, there could
be no other than the maestro's bride.

It is treason to hurt or maim molten
swans—played each key with firm finality
and to one soul it resounded teary
into eternity, her one stolen
perfume, that languishing fragrance of youth
when she brought a young blond runaway home
and let her sleep on the couch like a poem
for a few hours into morning. Uncouth,
we lifted our heads in the corn fields, dark
eyes watched a girl running in a sundress
until tears streamed down our faces, music
this beautiful is the texture of bark
on an oak tree, no longer are you less
for living vicariously, physic.

There is one remedy, lest you drive a
swan to its death. There are a host of tar-
black tutus that to the wood ballet barre
exact a plié in sequence, a way
a candle in the wind's brass bell rings it,
built up to its highest goals' aptitude,
eventually dies in solitude.
She first bends supple, like a grey cygnet,
in imitation of the older dance,
wrinkled seeds, dancers who have come before,
deep in the ground were rooted and flawless.
Spoken word grows to a thousand's applause,
green Earth's oldest tree could not be deformed,
subtle rejection grew its desert claws.

On the dun outskirts of society,
she had suffered every rejection known
to humankind, there was no more wind-blown
morality to impropriety.
Was she now oil or wine, the verse would look;
and the vineyard ran purple with royal
colours, the swollen grapes bursting from toil,
the ground was sandstone and red underfoot.
It was night; the young woman, olive tow'rd,
the sun's star was far gone at eleven—
in cape, she rang the bell. There was silence.
She would come again, there would be power—
reciting by heart an emollient;
she would speak without seeing violence.

A swan's concerted effort at swimming
is made to look quite effortless, seeming
a quiet glide through waters deep, reaming
at a classroom of old notions, dimming
lanterns with olive oil, lighting the way
by new commitments and new trust in love
that makes us human, singular above
dependency and mentoring our stay
on earth here for awhile: we are alive,
we felt pain, and knew what it was to be
swans and sacrifice for what we believed
in. We went hungry, were unrealized,
we fed the children of tomorrow, sea-
swept lives full of memories, now retrieved.

Requiem of the Lilith

Her flower was the lily, ominous
white, that spoke of pale stones left by moonlight,
when the toppled spades landed on the might
of what we call home, writing, venomous.
There was a churchyard, yet all was still now,
and by the darkness's dread came Lilith fair;
they thought her but a witch and yet ensnared
by her enchantments, verse and rhyme they bow.
Her hair was fiery strawberry blond, to
the waxen marble floor. When by the fence
there came a herd of Jersey cows, and she
called them, and their bells jangling, they came through
the gate into the churchyard. The spire lent
its shadow to the falling light, and lea.

There was a glad flower, men in a bind—
if it were real or imagined; yet nigh,
it produced the most frightful velvet kythe,
hallucinations of another kind,
and no one knew their meaning until dreams
were interpreted by those of the art.
They woke from their starry beds with a start
and could not discern if their nightmares, cream
of another chocolate from the night's fist.
The problem was that peasants were so tight
with their coins that they could not entertain
royalty. Yet Lilith summoned all, list
in royal procession, walking down bright
aisle with swaths of innocent gown and train.

The Lilith was a beauteous blond curl
that wrapped its way around her platinum
coronet, the head whose skull was mamon
and yet ivory. Her ash produced pearl,
yet only one drop, for the inner scent
of transcendence had wreathed her to the earth
her dying day, when on a pyre of mirth
she lay. The clothing of the trees was rent
to autumn's scarlet mood, and bounteous
sepia scarves, in colours of the weave.
She wore Eve's clothing yet, adorned in sun's
gold rings that haloed her; now humorous
she glanced in the mirror of the lake's eve
and knew the moments of the fairy's pun.

There was a time in the beginning when
all earth had bowed to her regality,
her mind with Adam's knew equality,
her mode had been his decent soul mate then.
Yet, when she would not marry him in moons
and acquiesced only to the wood's haunt,
she fell short of all his desires, his wont
for a mother of children, that blue womb
submitted to the throne of his mindful
patriarchy, his husbandry, his care;
when she would not bear his children, her cool
black eyes flashed at him lightning's silver foil…
the tresses of her head laid golden bare,
and with her mouth she kissed him as a fool.

Her power would be in her aloneness,
the desert of her hands without fruit ripe—
crimson from lime—her stateliness a gripe
she would take from the ancient gnarled fruitless
mossy tree, growing from the beginning
of the world to the end of time, purple
starless, casting shadows of its cripple
who embarrassed it too, leaving a line
of shame. She would leave, then, and make self stilled,
scarce amongst the rocks and grey caverns stone
of the desert. Her planet, colourless
was another space, where no being dwelled
save the remnants of Isaiah, alone
with his parchment scroll, rolled here effortless.

There we would find her, quiet as the sand
under the moon, in a desert of owls
where only jackals hide. This was her fowl,
the birds of the air she called by name, and
they followed through skies of dusty Hades
in train, as if the light has held them there.
It was the end, she was the thief, and bare
his hand, he would, for his last card, of spades,
was dark Lilith. They feared her in the night
as was her way, with black claws and fearsome
beak. They pulled the shades, they held their children
close, yet they had called upon her midnight
with frightening incantations, winsome
wiles and treacherous prayers to euthendom.

Was there an end to this ghostly story?
The moons swirled, and rings of planets turned to
silver, yet there was only one thorough
woman dark, one—alone in her pouring
called a heaven of hell, was this necklace.
Diamonds of its setting glimmered power,
in the shallows of seas, fish like flowers
swam silver before the throne of clear glass:
he who sits at the bottom of the Great
River watched it all. He knew Lilith from
of old, and watched her hair meld with the gold
sunsets of men's minds. Manicured estate
stretched to the wrought iron fence in green dun.
New York: this was the city of dreams run.

Requiem of the Siren

That was my golden hair, similitude
to past enchantments and Persephone,
conducting the blending aquamarine
with flashing heads, spirited dolphins' broods
with pools of tide, fragmented sea-scored shell
that broke the wave upon the shore of death:
a carcass of the whale was there in breadth,
the length of a ship, its past hulk of hell.
The symphony of water and earth vast
as the panorama of gemstone's fire
torments these blue lovers, bound in tumult
to future's marriage ring: no ending last,
hidden jewel of nature's cleft, to sire
their tryst with sea, and their poet, the salt.

Miranda was seen offshore in a storm,
the tempest was evidenced in the tide
of spray against the lighthouse, ghostly-eyed
in moonlight, through the wee hours of the morn.
A sun would rise, its reddened rays would pierce
fog of misperception, waiting for you:
become a conceptual woman, too
tired by the wind and its haze, coerced
no longer by manipulative hands,
the elements demand that you survive
in deference to them and their dark wails.
To the brine muse these were effortless rants,
she had no evil notions to contrive,
she effaced them with her green siren's tail.

In the depths beneath which the mer-castle
lay, there was a siren queen with refined
melodious lines and beings, benign
starfish fibula made wool oracles.
From a mermaid's nautilus shell emerged
in marine blue, carded yarn, like a dream.
The mermaids held her baby son supreme,
from the rule of Tristan not now submerged.
The queenly mother sang, harmonious
the salt waters drifted by, eventide
in laser cut brass and soft enamel:
whisperings of the seahorse to the gust
of salt and lash of navy. Sunset's bride:
moon will rise at twelve and ride in purple.

Deserts beneath the sea were sandy, coarse,
with scarlet crustaceans in number
to seduce those golden torn asunder
and the bottom's tap of thunder was remorse.
The conductor continued at the reigns
of the sea house deep beneath the turquoise;
it was a mermaid's lair and with my eyes
I saw the brittle castle's coral veins.
Flanked by equestrian horses in red,
I plumbed the deeps of oceanic bliss
and sky aglow with setting lucid teints.
O'er the cliffs the rival raptors circled.
I wore linen (and was of sea born lips),
highlights of my crown were ruby painted.

Let the beautiful marine chord resound—
O Linen: undertunic of the sand,
tri-coloured, penchant, hanging from the land;
our stitches have reclothed you, and we found
you hanging by a mermaid's silver thread.
The haggard stones of earth your tomb laid bare,
archaic doctrines speak of mermaid's lair,
the simple life of stone on stone for bed.
Their pillow lies beneath my head, for dire
is the hard life of those who work not play
for bread of kale, and crusty Irish moss.
The jewels of the mind and heart, the wire
therein the caverns of the sea doth weigh
of blood on fire. The eldest simple cloth.

Fine and unusual sleeves in garnet,
the embroidery meanders mouline,
pendants of magic and solstice earring
wear themes of the wind's silken clarinet.
This, your favourite white tunic—a dress
so long it would drag on the castle floor;
but executioner is at the door—
life is over with its clumsy caress.
He seeks a chopping of your golden locks;
his orders are clear: you'll have no trial.
You look already dressed in acclaim's bills
of mermaid songs and runes among the rocks,
the shores have woven memory in style,
linguist: but what is that to the lame hills.

Bright dominant chord sounds in ocean's nave,
each home of pearl-fringed shell is icy kind,
but is there not a tear behind the smile?
The sea is calling, knows your ancient cave.
The mer-Queen waits for Tristan to come home
each night by window roped in black velvet;
even though the stars are far away, sits
she by the casement, wary of his throne.
This bonnet in kind is made of fine lace,
is the baby's helmet and the sea salt
stirs. Rivers of the deep flow, currents down,
where Medea pours oils upon the face
of beggarly poor who heavenward call—
salt mines of poetry beneath the ground.

Requiem of the Waterflower

Under the weeping willow, embedded
with opulent pearl, for eternity—
silk and cotton now momentarily
to the floor, the mossy river threaded
through the countryside ambling on at rest.
The long draped wing-like creamy bell-shaped sleeves
hung, momentous and old as the dry leaves
upon the ground. The guests dressed in their best
were unsure whether they were here, gifting
for a moment or a new century,
as the water floated by, the petals
met reflection of the hills, now sloping
away into the distance, luxury
of the crescent moon still whitened, natal.

It's rare to be so quiet at deep grooves
that the moon, still unborn, whispers loudly
amid the bustle of skirts, with baby
carriages, and swish of dark horses hooves.
It's rare to have a bluest heart so kind
that one would flutter in midair over
the stained purple-white wild lilies cover.
There was a greenish bank where diamond rinds,
hues of bubbles floated, amid stoic
remembrances and florid faces, sound
as glassy-eyed wine. The only priest was
present in season of the Spring Fair, it
cantered like a new horse, as he came 'round
only twice per year when given good cause.

The bride was wearing white soft-spoken lace,
her ladies, blue willowy glass figures,
baby's breath to roses. Dainty creatures
of a delicate nature, they made case
that her figure was a pale rose in bloom
and her soft creases did not hide a child,
shining gold hair was plaited, smooth and mild,
she was quite reverent of his duty too.
But she was kind, and timely amid strife,
life in its piercing the dank moss shallows
of her life had made them crisp flowing pools,
and she stretched out her hand, became a wife,
she wore the diamond of her days, fallows
of a fertile land, farmed with ancient tools.

This royal moment in the river field
acquiesced to nature's horn and plenty,
no woman's life should be poor and wanting;
translucent gown following and men reeled
at the sight of such a character to
stand so graceful and so elegant, mild
as would a maiden be, yet there with child,
as her bourgeoning soul would attest, blue
were his eyes, and theirs was a renaissance
ceremony, in formal dress, as spoke
the custom of their age. They were not young,
too young, to be the green reconnaissance
of all love in youthful years, which day woke
too early—was it just the web was spun?

The matchmaker nodded her fair consent,
they had breathed vows, a renaissance couple,
common in their time, even nuptials
were seen in almost half of cream crescent
moon young lovers wed along shadowed lull
of waters, where the trim of flowers deck
while perfectly gathered at the scooped neck,
and the pearl beaded bodice falls below
the wedding full of fine giving detail,
a life joined to a life is turtledoves—
where no death, waxen, cold, where flaxen breathes
the clothed bridesmaids celebrate, holding train.
The vests of his men were as brown as cloves,
velvet, and marching on in league motifs.

It was the Golden Age of Art Nouveau:
the curved glass bell of time had rung before—
mosaics out of brokenness, stained cores
of glass rose from marble floor to dome, no
sinewy sense of movement was nature's
graceful shapes paired with yellowed narcissus.
The time of falling dusk had walked with us
into the organic future that spurs
the art of a new century, detail
fine and ornamental in its finite
way of climbing intricate design walk
of the nineteenth century with black rail
to render elements sculptural wine,
fluent in curves, iris buds and starched stalks.

How had this composite of medieval
times, limber of foot, danced into black tie
irony with exotic butterfly,
as was the case of her entourage belles.
There was the artist, the model a muse
sitting pale, simple before the painter—
no movement, hands folded, as in winter
of a soul, a childless stance waiting, loose
of the trappings of work and menial
blank servitude that so characterized
the eyes of darkened blind without new art;
here, the dim room started, congenial
to be receptive to old sterilized
forms of dying while still alive, thou art.

A Townswoman's Cloak

The vase would be for the yellow sun-streaked
daffodil, its brilliant bouquet untold
in hues, Wales aristocracy of gold
under the watch of gothic castles, meek
out of gentle song of a thousand trees
next to black international velvet.
Where the spires rise to the morn's fiery stealth
the ink drawing can scarcely describe me
as I am now, my hair white, my eyes bright,
I am in waiting as the country's sight
is just out of reach too. The stone upon
stone of Caernarfon and Harlech's dim light
seeping out from walls within walls and tide
waters brimming far away dreamy shore.

There is light in this vase of yellow-born,
like the sun streaming across the miles, bold
and high cliffs, isolated nature, old
red sandstone, rugged cliffs battered by storms,
wild grass hosting a long Skokholm haven:
seabirds, in heath and salt marsh, St. John's wort
rises serene; three-lobed water crowfoot—
with whisper of dew on ancient heaven.
In the grassland there are the tree mallow,
small nettle, sea campion—the guillemots,
chiffchaff, willow warblers, common whitethroat,
over mudstones and Red Maris. Fallow,
the linen of the garment lay in knots,
and the seamstress laboured at the new cloak.

With yellow dress now tied at her thin waist,
lace enamel lapping at her pale sleeves,
the ties drew back the bodice, and the lea
glistened from beyond her locked garden gate.
Ghostly was the sound of rabbits footsteps,
quietly the dawn transpired its gold knock;
the meadow courted her favour, as clock
ticked on and guided her elder years, debt
to those who had shown her guidance, advice
over the years always wise with graying
mentors's speech, their moment joys and shadows,
until she knelt with sentiment, chastised.
In the will of God: saints—deepest praying—
stone upon stone was an altar hallowed.

The moor, grasslands and coast, rife with curlew:
eerily they call, and townspeople lift
their heads—shaking at the suicide rifts
which rise to sky and echo; almost rue
their grey feathered existence were they not
shrieking a blood-chilling eloquent call,
frightening as Eden's vine at the Fall,
her austere fertility entwined brought
images of fruit and flow'r to the mind,
along with temptress of the gnarled tree,
where pressure from the dark side stormy, breaks
down walls of the imagination-kind.
Pecking in the mud with icy curved beaks
each curlew contrasts Snowdon's snow-flaked peak.

ENDNOTES

Section 1: Medieval Apothecary

The Apothecary's Daughter 14 Poem re-published from *Hallmark: Canada's 150 Year Anniversary* (Dove Christian Publishing, 2017) p. 304.

Section 2: Old Poets

Battersea Bridge 20 Poem re-published from *The Fleur-de-lis* (Tate Publishing, 2011) 'Ode to Enchantment" Vol I, p.113. *Contains reference to journal entry from Ruth Pitter from the book C. S. Lewis, Poet by Don King, p.226.*

Laughter at Oxford 21 Poem re-published from *The Fleur-de-lis* (Tate Publishing, 2011) 'Ode to Enchantment" Vol I, p.114.

To An Aged Don 22 Poem re-published from *The Fleur-de-lis* (Tate Publishing, 2011) 'Ode to Enchantment" Vol I, p.115. *Phrase in quotes, contains reference to C.S Lewis from the book C. S. Lewis, Poet by Don King, p.224.*

Of a War 23 Poem re-published from *The Fleur-de-lis* (Tate Publishing, 2011) 'Ode to Enchantment" Vol I, p.116.

Crown of Thorns 24 Poem re-published from *The Fleur-de-lis* (Tate Publishing, 2011) 'Ode to Enchantment" Vol I, p.117.

Meditations in a Flame 25 Poem re-published from *The Fleur-de-lis* (Tate Publishing, 2011) 'Ode to Enchantment" Vol I, p.118.

Eye of the Storm 26 Poem re-published from *The Fleur-de-lis* (Tate Publishing, 2011) 'Ode to Enchantment" Vol I, p.119.

Quill and Ink 27 Poem re-published from *The Fleur-de-lis* (Tate Publishing, 2011) 'Ode to Enchantment" Vol I, p.120.

In Prison 28 Poem re-published from *The Fleur-de-lis* (Tate Publishing, 2011) 'Ode to Enchantment" Vol I, p.121.

Emeritus 29 Poem re-published from *The Fleur-de-lis* (Tate Publishing, 2011) 'Ode to Enchantment" Vol I, p.122.

Walk Amongst the Shrines 30 Poem re-published from *The Fleur-de-lis* (Tate Publishing, 2011) 'Ode to Enchantment" Vol I, p.123.

The River 31 Poem re-published from *The Fleur-de-lis* (Tate Publishing, 2011) 'Ode to Enchantment" Vol I, p.125.

Farm Boy 32 Poem re-published from *The Fleur-de-lis* (Tate Publishing, 2011) 'Ode to Enchantment" Vol I, p.126.

Chronicle 33 Poem re-published from *The Fleur-de-lis* (Tate Publishing, 2011) 'Ode to Enchantment" Vol I, p.127.

Caravan 34 Poem re-published from *The Fleur-de-lis* (Tate Publishing, 2011) 'Ode to Enchantment" Vol I, p.128.

Bombs and Gallows 35 Poem re-published from *The Fleur-de-lis* (Tate Publishing, 2011) 'Ode to Enchantment" Vol I, p.129.

Shetland Pony 36 Poem re-published from *The Fleur-de-lis* (Tate Publishing, 2011) 'Ode to Enchantment" Vol I, p.130.

Gold Vermilion 37 Poem re-published from *The Fleur-de-lis* (Tate Publishing, 2011) 'Ode to Enchantment" Vol I, p.131.

Dante 38 Poem re-published from *The Fleur-de-lis* (Tate Publishing, 2011) 'Ode to Enchantment" Vol I, p.132.

Motet 39 Poem re-published from *The Fleur-de-lis* (Tate Publishing, 2011) 'Ode to Enchantment" Vol I, p.133.

Valentine Raptures 40 Poem re-published from *The Fleur-de-lis* (Tate Publishing, 2011) 'Ode to Enchantment" Vol I, p.134.

Ballet 41 Poem re-published from *The Fleur-de-lis* (Tate Publishing, 2011) 'Ode to Enchantment" Vol I, p.135.

The Poet 42 Poem re-published from *The Fleur-de-lis* (Tate Publishing, 2011) 'Ode to Enchantment" Vol I, p.137.

The Bread 43 Poem re-published from *The Fleur-de-lis* (Tate Publishing, 2011) 'Ode to Enchantment" Vol I, p.138.

Acacia 44 Poem re-published from *The Fleur-de-lis* (Tate Publishing, 2011) 'Ode to Enchantment" Vol I, p.139.

Pale Lights 45 Poem re-published from *The Fleur-de-lis* (Tate Publishing, 2011) 'Ode to Enchantment" Vol I, p.140.

Old Worlds 46 Poem re-published from *The Fleur-de-lis* (Tate Publishing, 2011) 'Ode to Enchantment" Vol I, p.141.

Other Suns 47 Poem re-published from *The Fleur-de-lis* (Tate Publishing, 2011) 'Ode to Enchantment" Vol I, p.142.

Other Galaxies 48 Poem re-published from *The Fleur-de-lis* (Tate Publishing, 2011) 'Ode to Enchantment" Vol I, p.143.

Chrysanthemum 50 Poem re-published from *The Fleur-de-lis* (Tate Publishing, 2011) 'Ode to Enchantment" Vol I, p.145.

Stone Fortress 51 Poem re-published from *The Fleur-de-lis* (Tate Publishing, 2011) 'Ode to Enchantment" Vol I, p.146 .

Hearth Fire 52 Poem re-published from *The Fleur-de-lis* (Tate Publishing, 2011) 'Ode to Enchantment" Vol I, p.147.

Shining Armour 53 Poem re-published from *The Fleur-de-lis* (Tate Publishing, 2011) 'Ode to Enchantment" Vol I, p.148.

Section 4: Isaacson's Last Hour

Hourglass 68. Poem re-published from *Victoriana* (The Emily Isaacson Institute, 2015) p.22.

Love Poem of the Lily 69. Poem re-published from *Victoriana* (The Emily Isaacson Institute, 2015) p.23.

Butterfly Tears 70. Poem re-published from *Victoriana* (The Emily Isaacson Institute, 2015) p.24 .

Threnody of the Thistle 71 Poem re-published from *Victoriana* (The Emily Isaacson Institute, 2015) p.25.

Canon of Bloom 72 Poem re-published from *Victoriana* (The Emily Isaacson Institute, 2015) p.26.

Burning Cinders 73 Poem re-published from *Victoriana* (The Emily Isaacson Institute, 2015) p.27.

Dirge of the Daffodil 74 Poem re-published from *Victoriana* (The Emily Isaacson Institute, 2015) p.28.

Idyll of the Iris 75 Poem re-published from *Victoriana* (The Emily Isaacson Institute, 2015) p.29.

True Lace of Ireland (found poem) 76 Poem re-published from *Victoriana* (The Emily Isaacson Institute, 2015) p.30. Original work is a magazine article from Victoria Magazine (Hoffman Media) on Kenmare Lace. Found poem.

A Daffodil In Wales 77 Poem re-published from *Victoriana* (The Emily Isaacson Institute, 2015) p.31.

Elegy of the Royal Rose 78 Poem re-published from *Victoriana* (The Emily Isaacson Institute, 2015) p.32.

Section 5: Letters From the Peace Tower

The Forest's Weave 79 Poem re-published from *House of Rain* (Potter's Press, 2016) p.11.

Pedigree 80 Poem re-published from *House of Rain* (Potter's Press, 2016) p. 12.

Last Light 81 Poem re-published from *House of Rain* (Potter's Press, 2016) p.13.

The Horizon's Muse 82 Poem re-published from *House of Rain* (Potter's Press, 2016) p.14.

The Replanting 83 Poem re-published from *House of Rain* (Potter's Press, 2016) p.15.

I Held A Lantern By The Sea 84 Poem re-published from *House of Rain* (Potter's Press, 2016) p.17.

The Metropolitan Sun 85 Poem re-published from *House of Rain* (Potter's Press, 2016) p.24.

Enclosure 86 Poem re-published from *House of Rain* (Potter's Press, 2016) p.19.

Cultivation Of The Olive Tree 87 Poem re-published from *House of Rain* (Potter's Press, 2012) p.20.

Section 6: The Pigeons

A Street of Many Doors 88 Poem re-published from *Hallmark: Canada's 150 Year Anniversary* (Dove Christian Publishing, 2017) p.42.

A House of Many Walls 89 Poem re-published from *Hallmark: Canada's 150 Year Anniversary* (Dove Christian Publishers, 2017) p.44.

Emerging Sparrows and Salt 91 Poem re-published from *Hallmark: Canada's 150 Year Anniversary* (Dove Christian Publishers, 2017) p.317.

For a Dying Crown 96-7. Reference to quote:"That is what happens to totalitarian movements and death cults once the spell is broken and their official narratives fall apart. When they go down, they try to take the whole world with them." CJ Hopkins, The Last Days of the Covidian Cult. January 18, 2022. (Published online as "For A Dying Ukrainian Crown").

Section 7: Clay Hearts

A Catholic Star 100 Poem re-published from *Hallmark: Canada's 150 Year Anniversary* (Dove Christian Publishers, 2017) p.294-295.

Midnight in the Street 102 Poem re-published from *Hallmark: Canada's 150 Year Anniversary* (Dove Christian Publishers, 2017) p.296-297.

The Weeping Branch 104 Poem re-published from *Hallmark: Canada's 150 Year Anniversary* (Dove Christian Publishers, 2017) p.298.

Section 8: Dogwood Manor

Dogwood Crest 105 Poem re-published from *Hallmark: Canada's 150 Year Anniversary* (Dove Christian Publishers, 2017) p.4.

Spiritual Touch 107 Poem re-published *The Fleur-de-lis*, Vol III Tate Publishing, 2011), p.95-96.

A New Valley 110 Poem re-published from *Hallmark: Canada's 150 Year Anniversary* (Dove Christian Publishers, 2017) p.11-12.

Time for a Poet 112 Poem re-published from *Hallmark: Canada's 150 Year Anniversary* (Dove Christian Publishers, 2017) p.14-16

This Is Where You Keep Me 115 Poem re-published from *Hallmark: Canada's 150 Year Anniversary* (Dove Christian Publishers, 2017) p.20-24.

Section 9: A History of Temperance

Historical Hurricane 120 Poem re-published from *Hallmark: Canada's 150 Year Anniversary* (Dove Christian Publishers, 2017) p.28.

What the Lilac Was Not 121 Poem re-published from *Hallmark: Canada's 150 Year Anniversary* (Dove Christian Publishers, 2017) p.29.

A Little Fury 122 Poem re-published from *Hallmark: Canada's 150 Year Anniversary* (Dove Christian Publishers, 2017) p.30.

In Relevant Cards 123 Poem re-published from *Hallmark: Canada's 150 Year Anniversary* (Dove Christian Publishers, 2017) p.31.

Petrified Wood 124 Poem re-published from *Hallmark: Canada's 150 Year Anniversary* (Dove Christian Publishers, 2017) p.32.

Apples of Gold in Settings of Silver 125 Poem re-published from *Hallmark: Canada's 150 Year Anniversary* (Dove Christian Publishers, 2017) p.33. *Title refers to a verse from the Bible: "a word fitly spoken is like apples of gold in settings of silver." Proverbs 25:11 KJV*

Reservoir Blue 126 Poem re-published from *Hallmark: Canada's 150 Year Anniversary* (Dove Christian Publishers, 2017) p.34.

Breathing Space 127 Poem re-published from *Hallmark: Canada's 150 Year Anniversary* (Dove Christian Publishers, 2017) p.35.

View of Mount Song 128 Poem re-published from *Hallmark: Canada's 150 Year Anniversary* (Dove Christian Publishers, 2017) p.36.

In the Custody of Angels 130 Poem re-published from *Hallmark: Canada's 150 Year Anniversary* (Dove Christian Publishers, 2017) p.37.

Section 10: Recession Icons

Beside the Golden Door 131 Poem re-published from *Hallmark: Canada's 150 Year Anniversary* (Dove Christian Publishers, 2017) p.40
   Quote 1 : "The New Colossus" by Emma Lazarus. 1 Pub. 1883 [public domain].
   Quote 2: "Brother Can You Spare A Dime" General Domain. Quote is title of famous song of the Great Depression, "Brother Can You Spare A Dime?" sung by Bing Crosby. Songwriters E. Y. Harburg / Jay Gorney. Lyrics © 1932 Warner Chappell Music, Inc, Next Decade Entertainment, Inc.

The Little Match Girl 133 Poem re-published from *Hallmark: Canada's 150 Year Anniversary* (Dove Christian Publishers, 2017) p.53. Title celebrated a re-telling of the original story by Hans Christian Andersen, published in 1845.

A Second June 134 Poem re-published from *Hallmark: Canada's 150 Year Anniversary* (Dove Christian Publishers, 2017) p.41.

A Third April 135 Poem re-published from *Hallmark: Canada's 150 Year Anniversary* (Dove Christian Publishers, 2017) p.43.

Sky Wreath 136 Poem re-published from *Hallmark: Canada's 150 Year Anniversary* (Dove Christian Publishers, 2017) p.48.

Dreamscape Gray 137 Poem re-published from *Hallmark: Canada's 150 Year Anniversary* (Dove Christian Publishers, 2017) p.49.

My Little Black Book 138 Poem re-published from *Hallmark: Canada's 150 Year Anniversary* (Dove Christian Publishers, 2017) p.50.

Section 11: Swan Drum

Sonnet of Tears 139 Poem re-published from *Hallmark: Canada's 150 Year Anniversary* (Dove Christian Publishers, 2017) p.121.

Jacob's Ladder 140 Poem re-published from *Victoriana* (The Emily Isaacson Institute, 2015) p.32.

Salty Purse 141 Poem re-published from *Victoriana* (The Emily Isaacson Institute, 2015) p.32.

Vintage Lamp 142 Poem re-published from *Victoriana* (The Emily Isaacson Institute, 2015) p.32.

Spikenard Madonna 143 Poem re-published from *Victoriana* (The Emily Isaacson Institute, 2015) p.32.

Cherry Trees in Blossom 144 Poem re-published from *Victoriana* (The Emily Isaacson Institute, 2015) p.32.

Section 12: Sonnet Potpourri

The light shone out a little bleary-eyed, 154 Poem re-published from *Hallmark: Canada's 150 Year Anniversary* (Dove Christian Publishers, 2017) p.151.

When I have lived my years, I shall recall 155 Poem re-published from *Hallmark: Canada's 150 Year Anniversary* (Dove Christian Publishers, 2017) p.152.

When I would give my parting glance to thee, 156 Poem re-published from *Hallmark: Canada's 150 Year Anniversary* (Dove Christian Publishers, 2017) p.156.

City of flowers, sweet moments at will, 157 Poem re-published from *Hallmark: Canada's 150 Year Anniversary* (Dove Christian Publishers, 2017) p.157.

Lovely, my lovely when the night has passed, 158 Poem re-published from *Hallmark: Canada's 150 Year Anniversary* (Dove Christian Publishers, 2017) p.158.

Soldier-like, bravest man a rising moon—159 Poem re-published from *Hallmark: Canada's 150 Year Anniversary* (Dove Christian Publishers, 2017) p.159. Eclipsed poem co-written with Victor's Hugo's play "Hernani" (General Domain). The Works of Victor Hugo: One Volume Edition. (Walter J. Black, Inc., 1928), 777.

Now to my end I come in stately black, 160 Poem re-published from *Hallmark: Canada's 150 Year Anniversary* (Dove Christian Publishers, 2017) p.181.

Your last word in this pallid hospice realm 162 Poem re-published from *Hallmark: Canada's 150 Year Anniversary* (Dove Christian Publishers, 2017) p.171.

O flame that circles me—O wisdom's light, 163 Poem re-published from *Hallmark: Canada's 150 Year Anniversary* (Dove Christian Publishers, 2017) p.183.

Section 13: Oblique Doors

Dimes 164 Poem re-published from *Hallmark: Canada's 150 Year Anniversary* (Dove Christian Publishers, 2017) p.188.

Newsprint 165 Poem re-published from *Hallmark: Canada's 150 Year Anniversary* (Dove Christian Publishers, 2017) p.189.

Small and Shy 166 Poem re-published from *Hallmark: Canada's 150 Year Anniversary* (Dove Christian Publishers, 2017) p.190.

Rugged 167 Poem re-published from *Hallmark: Canada's 150 Year Anniversary* (Dove Christian Publishers, 2017) p.191.

One Minute Per House 168 Poem re-published from *Hallmark: Canada's 150 Year Anniversary* (Dove Christian Publishers, 2017) p.192.

Early Light 169 Poem re-published from *Hallmark: Canada's 150 Year Anniversary* (Dove Christian Publishers, 2017) p.193.

Wages 170 Poem re-published from *Hallmark: Canada's 150 Year Anniversary* (Dove Christian Publishers, 2017) p.194.

Mundane 171 Poem re-published from *Hallmark: Canada's 150 Year Anniversary* (Dove Christian Publishers, 2017) p.195.

Misfit 172 Poem re-published from *Hallmark: Canada's 150 Year Anniversary* (Dove Christian Publishers, 2017) p.196.

News Copy 173 Poem re-published from *Hallmark: Canada's 150 Year Anniversary* (Dove Christian Publishers, 2017) p.197.

Olive Oil 174 Poem re-published from *Hallmark: Canada's 150 Year Anniversary* (Dove Christian Publishers, 2017) p.198.

Section 14: Oil of Heaven

Call to the Poets (Fantasia) 175 Poem re-published from *Hallmark: Canada's 150 Year Anniversary* (Dove Christian Publishers, 2017) p.216-217.

Monarch in the Subway (Da capo aria) 177 Poem re-published from *Hallmark: Canada's 150 Year Anniversary* (Dove Christian Publishers, 2017) p.224-225.

I Heard the Owl Call My Name (Pasticcio) 179 Poem re-published from *Hallmark: Canada's 150 Year Anniversary* (Dove Christian Publishers, 2017) p.226. *I Heard the Owl Call My Name* is a best-selling 1967 novel by Margaret Craven. The book tells the story of a young Anglican vicar named Mark Brian who, unbeknownst to him, has not long to live. He learns about the meaning of life when he is to be sent to a First Nations parish in British Columbia

Still Learning You (Verismo) 181 Poem re-published from *Hallmark: Canada's 150 Year Anniversary* (Dove Christian Publishers, 2017) p.228.

Acknowledgement (Ossia) 183 Poem re-published from *Hallmark: Canada's 150 Year Anniversary* (Dove Christian Publishers, 2017) p.229.

Section 15: Humanitarian Objections

The Shoe Tree 184 Poem re-published from *Hallmark: Canada's 150 Year Anniversary* (Dove Christian Publishers, 2017) p.232-233

Dragons in the Swamp 186 Poem re-published from *Hallmark: Canada's 150 Year Anniversary* (Dove Christian Publishers, 2017) p.234

Dragons in the Caves 187 Poem re-published from *Hallmark: Canada's 150 Year Anniversary* (Dove Christian Publishers, 2017) p.235.

Before the Fire 188 Poem re-published from *Hallmark: Canada's 150 Year Anniversary* (Dove Christian Publishers, 2017) p.236-237.

The Cupboard 190 Poem re-published from *Hallmark: Canada's 150 Year Anniversary* (Dove Christian Publishers, 2017) p.238-239.

If I Was Frost 192 Poem re-published from *Hallmark: Canada's 150 Year Anniversary* (Dove Christian Publishers, 2017) p.242-243.

The Fading Town 194 Poem re-published from *Hallmark: Canada's 150 Year Anniversary* (Dove Christian Publishers, 2017) p.244-245.

Weep Salt 196 Poem re-published from *Hallmark: Canada's 150 Year Anniversary* (Dove Christian Publishers, 2017) p.247.

Section 16: Ballads

Last Words From A Weaver's Basket 197 Poem re-published from *Hallmark: Canada's 150 Year Anniversary* (Dove Christian Publishers, 2017) p. 270.

Ballad of the Oboe Player 200 Poem re-published from *Hallmark: Canada's 150 Year Anniversary* (Dove Christian Publishers, 2017) p.273.

Section 17: Earth Talks to her Creator

The Evolution of Covid 205 Poem contains quote p 220 (4;3) that refers to the book *Lord of the Flies*, William Golding. Original quote: "Kill the pig. Cut her throat. Spill her blood." (Golding 72). This is an example of pastiche, a postmodern device.

Section 18: When the Sky is Falling

Skyfall Sonnet 224 Poem re-published from *House of Rain* (Potter's Press, 2016) p.141.
The Altar 225 Poem re-published from *House of Rain* (Potter's Press, 2016) p.106.

Section 19: Requiems in the Mist

Requiem of the Siren 254 "the simple life of stone on stone for bed./Their pillow lies beneath my head," quote refers to the book by Madeleine L'Engle, *A Stone for a Pillow*.